ViSUaL aRT
for the elementary classroom

Kerrian Neu

Writing, design and illustration by Kerrian Neu.

ISBN   1-45374-908-X
ISBN-13   978-1-453-74908-1

kerrian neu design
print/web design & illustration

www.tahoekerri.com
www.benthebee.com
www.evisualart.com
www.picturebookwriting.com

VISUAL ARTS TODAY.

Most agree that it is important to teach the visual arts, but what is really taught in the elementary classroom is mainly craft projects based on holidays and civic events. Students repeat what the teacher does, and little variation is accomplished.

Visual art is about expression and experimentation. Students work with differing media in their own way learn to use and create. It is best to show students how to use the media, but let them experiment and find their own method. Visual art creation is not about repeating what others do, it is about creating an individual style and work of art.

THE LESSONS.

The lessons of this book explore the elements of art and contain support materials and define art terms. Each grade has a series of lessons that build off each other and should be taught in order presented. The lessons also take into consideration California and Nevada visual art standards. The standards addressed for each lesson are in the back of this book.

ART JOURNALS.

An art journal is a part of most of the lessons and is a place for students to write reflections, definitions of art terms and sketch before drawing their final art piece. For kindergarten through grade one, each art journal should consist of the corresponding lesson reflecting pages (supplied at the end of each grade's lessons) and blank white paper for the students to draw/sketch. For grades two through five, each art journal should consist of 20 pages of lined paper and 10-20 pages of blank white paper. Stapled together and covered by a piece of white construction paper for the students to create their own colorful covers.

SUPPLEMENTAL MATERIALS.

The lessons that present artists also need pictures of the artist's work to show students. These supplemental (full color) pages are available for a free download and classroom use at www.eVisualArt.com.

Working with art media should be fun and easy. If you are unsure how to use any of them, experiment with the feel and flow of each before starting a lesson.

WATERCOLORS.
Watercolor pigments are used with water to dilute the pigment, allowing the painter to have the color flow across the paper. There are several methods to watercolor painting, the two most common techniques are called wet-on-wet and wet-on-dry. Wet-on-wet uses larger amounts of water, and the painter first wets the surface of the paper, then applies a damp pigment. Control can be difficult with this technique. Wet-on-dry is an easier technique to learn. The paper remains dry to start, and the pigment is applied with water. As a layer of paint dries, the painter can add depth and layers on top. The painter has more control of the pigment and detail in the painting.

PASTELS.
There are several types of pastels that can be used for the lessons of this book, soft pastels and oil pastels. Both work great on textured and colored papers.

Soft pastels are easy to blend and create colorful works of art. They have a feel similar to chalk and are sometimes called chalk pastels. They can be dusty, and a spray fixative should be used to prevent smudging of finished work. Blending of colors can be easily accomplished with tissues or cotton swabs.

Oil pastels have a more waxy, crayon feel and aren't as messy as soft pastels. They are also easy to work with, but blending is not as smooth. Oil pastels won't smudge as much as soft pastels, but still need a spray fixative.

TEMPERA.
Tempera is a great opaque paint. It shouldn't be diluted by water, and creates bright colorful paintings. Tempera works well for creating color wheels, and mixing colors, and it dries quickly.

The following pages are lesson plans for kindergarten. The lessons build off each other and include objectives, procedures, and supplies needed. Art journals should consist of blank paper to draw/sketch and lesson reflecting pages.

Objectives:
Students will learn about basic colors, identify objects that are those colors, cut and color object pages and assemble them into a color wheel.

Procedures:

1. Show objects that are red, orange, yellow, green, blue and purple, asking students to identify what color they each are. Also show how colors are arranged on a color wheel, and why the colors are in their locations. Display color wheel for all to see.

2. Pass out object coloring pages to students, (they can use crayons, oil pastels or tempera based on their abilities) asking students to color the object with it's associated color. Most of the object should be the main color.

3. After students have completed the coloring pages, have them carefully cut the objects out, and glue them onto a blank black or white paper, making a circle of the objects into a basic color wheel.

4. Have students choose a color, and draw an object associated with that color in their art journal, on the corresponding lesson page.

Supplies needed:
Art journal page, color wheel (available at www.evisualart.com), objects of basic colors, object coloring pages, black or white paper 12x18, crayons, oil pastels, or tempera, scissors, glue.

Name _____ Date _____

Name ______________________________ Date ________________

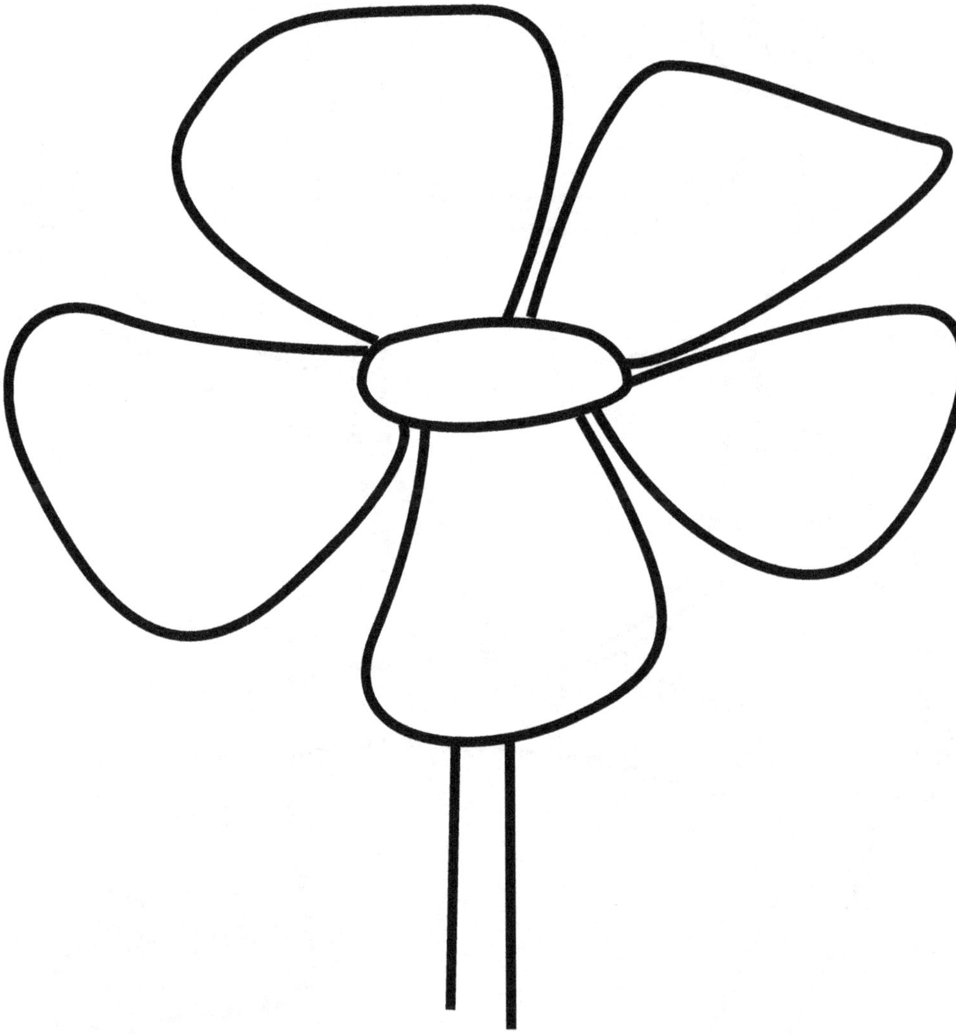

Name _____   Date _____

Name ______________________________ Date ______________

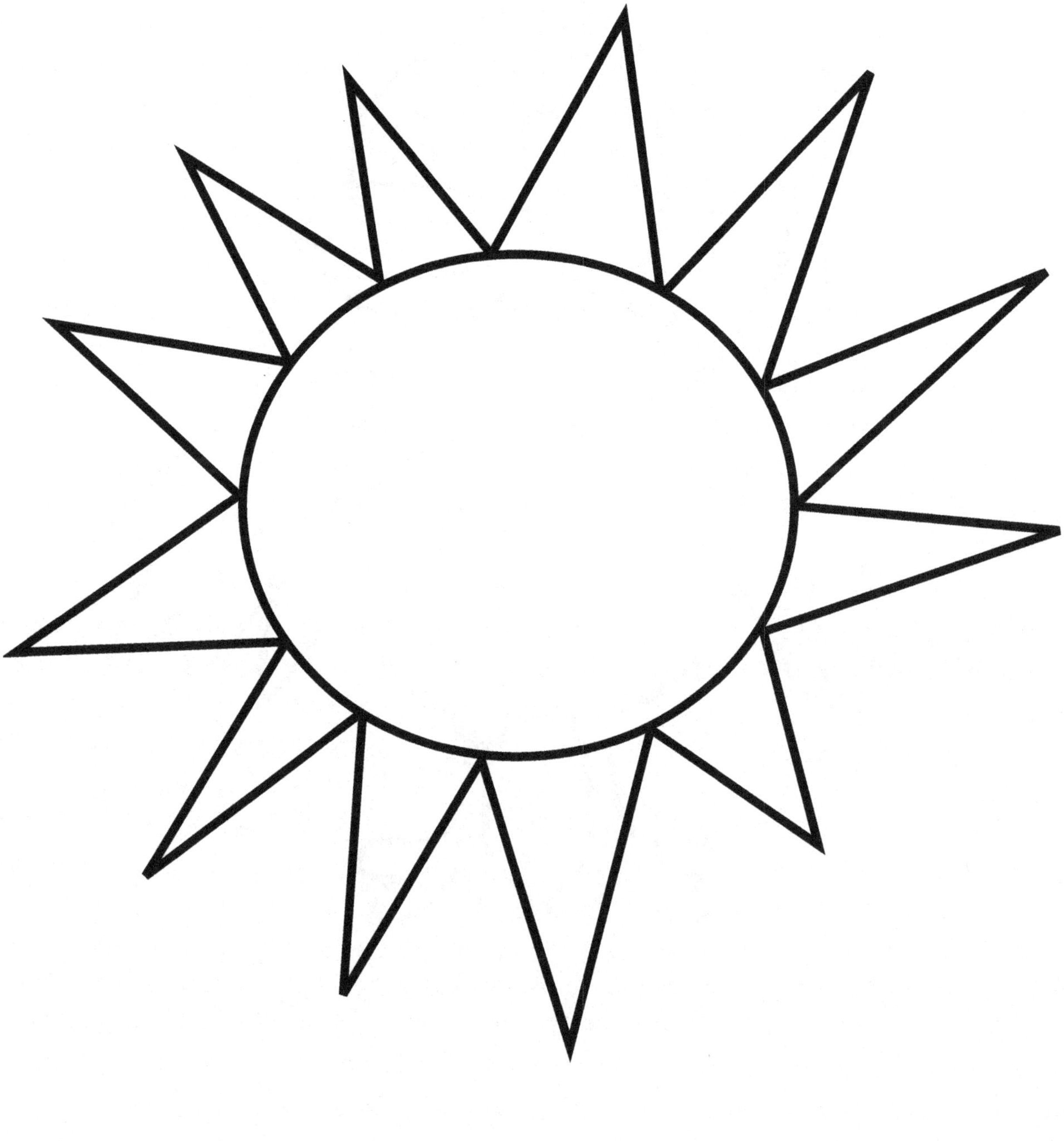

Name _____ Date _____

Name _____   Date _____

Objectives:

Students will learn to recognize basic shapes and create mobiles of basic shapes (circles, triangles, squares) and primary colors.

Procedures:

1. Ask students to observe objects throughout the classroom. Where do they see circles, squares and triangles?

2. Show students how to create the shapes with colored pipe cleaners tracing the shape they see on a paper.

3. Add varying lengths of string or fishing line and attach them to the shapes.

4. Hang the mobiles throughout the room.

5. Students reflect by drawing the shapes in their art journals.

Note: you can use cut paper shapes instead.

Supplies needed:

Art journal page, colorful pipe cleaners, string or fishing line.

grade
K   Lesson 2   Templates for Mobiles   page 14   VISUAL ART
                                                                            for the elementary classroom

Objectives:
Students will observe patterns and textures they see and feel in the environment and create caterpillars filled with textures.

Procedures:

1. Take students around the school, asking them to observe the patterns or textures they see. What shapes make up the patterns they see?

2. Demonstrate the method to creating a rubbing with rubbing plates or textures you find on ordinary objects (paper towels, fabrics, etc) and crayons (the side of a crayon works best).

3. Give students a large white paper, telling them to cover their whole paper with textures. They should use varying colors as well.

4. Once their paper is covered, have the students trace circles all over their paper, including one of a larger size. Students then cut out the circles.

5. Students glue the circles together, creating the body of a caterpillar. The larger circle creates the head.

6. Students add a face and legs to their caterpillar.

7. Students reflect on their creations by rubbing several textures in their art journals.

Supplies needed:
Art journal page, rubbing plates or flat objects with texture, crayons, white paper 12x18, circle templates, scissors, glue.

Name _____ Date _____

grade
K | Lesson 3 | Circle Templates for Caterpillars | page 16 | VISUAL ART
for the elementary classroom

Objectives:

Students will trace the steps of shapes, while playing musical shapes.

Procedures:

NOTE: Before beginning this lesson, create a pattern on the floor of large triangles, circles and squares using colored tape. Go around the whole room, or create several smaller patterns for smaller groups.

1. Explain the rules of the game to all students. Students must trace the shape of each object and then move to the next (once the previous student leaves it). One student (or the teacher) randomly spins the game wheel. The student announces "STOP" (each student stops on their shape) and then announces the shape and color. The student on that shape is out of the game. This goes on until their is only one student left.

2. Take turns playing the game.

3. Students reflect by drawing their own pattern in their art journals.

Supplies needed:

Art journal page, colored tape in red, orange, yellow, green, blue, purple, white and black, game spinner wheel (available at www.evisualart.com).

Objectives:

Students will use their knowledge of basic shapes to create 2-dimensional bugs of torn paper.

Procedures:

1. Go over basic shapes, drawing them on the board as students identify them.

2. Demonstrate how to tear paper into basic shapes. Give students a piece of paper to practice, making a square and a circle.

3. Ask students to identify the parts all bugs have (wings, eyes, legs, antenna, body, etc), writing them for all to see and use as a reference.

4. Using various colored papers, students create their own colorful bug, tearing the papers into the shapes for eyes, etc.

5. Students glue their bug onto a black paper.

6. Students share their bug, describing its parts and colors/shapes.

7. Students draw their bug in their art journal on the corresponding lesson page. (this step can be done before step 4)

Supplies needed:

Art journal page, colored papers, black paper 9x12 or larger, glue.

Objectives:
Students will use their 2D bugs to create a 3-dimensional bug.

Procedures:

1. Tell students that they are going to create a 3D bug that represents their 2D creation.

2. Discuss with students the rules of working with clay (no throwing, etc.), and have them put on aprons or other clothing to cover their clothes.

3. Place a large piece of paper for students to work on, protecting the table surface), and give each student some clay to work with. Allow them to work and play with it first before starting their bug.

4. Students view their 2D bug to help create their 3D bug. (Students can also do a new bug instead).

5. After the clay has dried, allow students to color their bug with markers, watercolors or tempera.

6. Students name their bug and reflect in their art journal which bug (2D or 3D) they like better and why.

Supplies needed:
Art journal page, 2D bug, clay, aprons, paper to cover tables, tempera, watercolors or markers to color the clay.

Objectives:
Students will trace ordinary objects creating an abstract collage of colors and shapes.

Procedures:

1. Demonstrate how to trace ordinary objects. Repeat the tracing over and over the paper, overlapping and rotating the object.

2. Give students white paper and an object to trace (e.g., scissors, compass) and have them repeat what you demonstrated.

3. After their tracing, students color in the spaces created in various colors, using a different color in each space created (not the overall original object).

4. Students share their creations, describing how they created it and what the object's everyday use is in their art journals.

Supplies needed:
Art journal page, watercolors, brushes, pencil to trace object, ordinary objects, white paper 9x12 or larger.

Objectives:
Students will learn about basic colors, identify objects that are those colors, cut and color object pages and assemble them into a color wheel.

Procedures:

1. Show objects that are red, orange, yellow, green, blue and purple, asking students to identify what color they each are. Also show how colors are arranged on a color wheel, and why the colors are in their locations. Display color wheel for all to see.

2. Pass out object coloring pages to students, (they can use crayons, oil pastels or tempera based on their abilities) asking students to color the object with it's associated color. Most of the object should be the main color.

3. After students have completed the coloring pages, have them carefully cut the objects out, and glue them onto a blank black or white paper, making a circle of the objects into a basic color wheel.

4. Students choose a color, and draw an object associated with that color in their art journal, on the corresponding lesson page.

Supplies needed:
Art journal page, color wheel, objects of basic colors, object coloring pages, black or white paper 12x18, crayons, oil pastels, or tempera, scissors, glue.

Name _____ Date _____

Name _____ Date _____

Name ______________________________ Date ______________

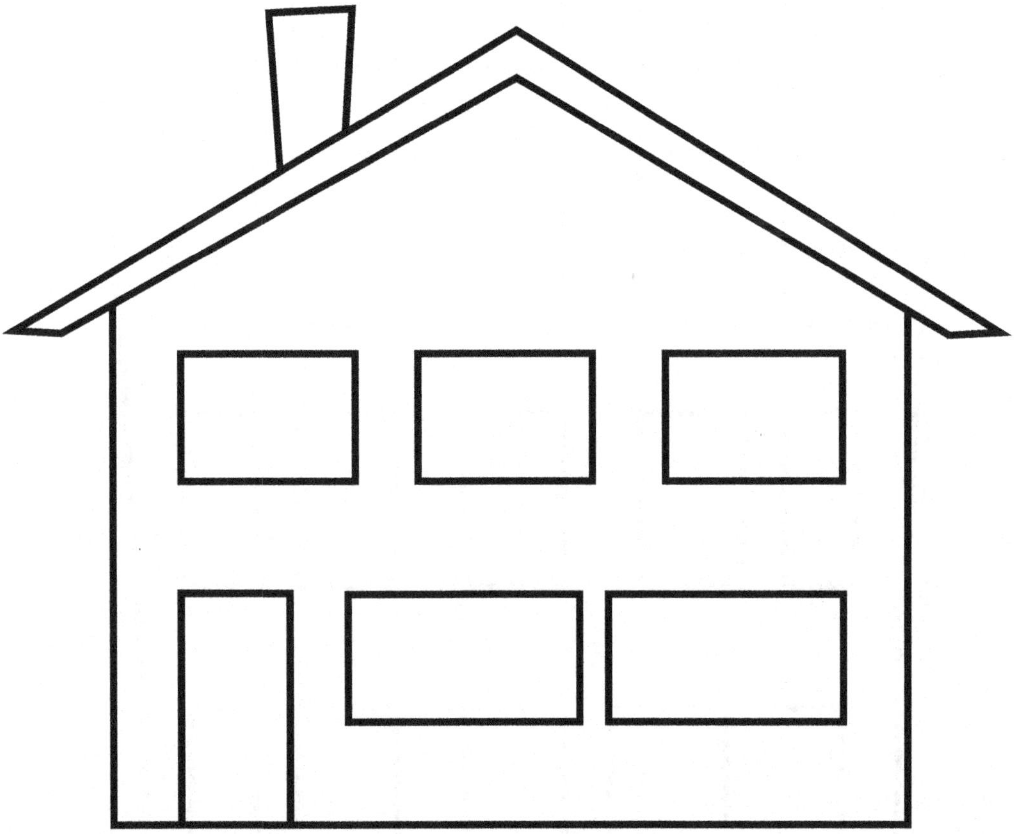

Objectives:
Students will create a town with buildings by creating buildings with patterns/textures, line and color.

Procedures:
1. Tell students that as a class, they are creating a town. Name the town, and while students are creating some buildings, make an area on a wall with a couple hills, water and roads to hold all the buildings. Student buildings will then be put up in the town.

2. Students create buildings (or use the templates supplied) for the town, using collage of papers, watercolors, tempera or crayon rubbings. The town needs skyscrapers and houses. Each building needs to have some pattern on it's walls (rubbings or patterns of shapes, e.g., bricks, wood).

3. Add each building to the town with the help of the students, allowing them some say in the placement.

4. Students reflect by drawing a copy of their building in their art journals.

Supplies needed:
Art journal page, building templates, white paper, watercolors, tempera, crayons, rubbing plates, scissors, area on a wall for the town, green and brown paper for the hills/mountains, blue for the water, gray/black for roads.

My Color: _____

My object:

Draw a circle, triangle and square.

My textures:
Keep each texture in the spaces below.

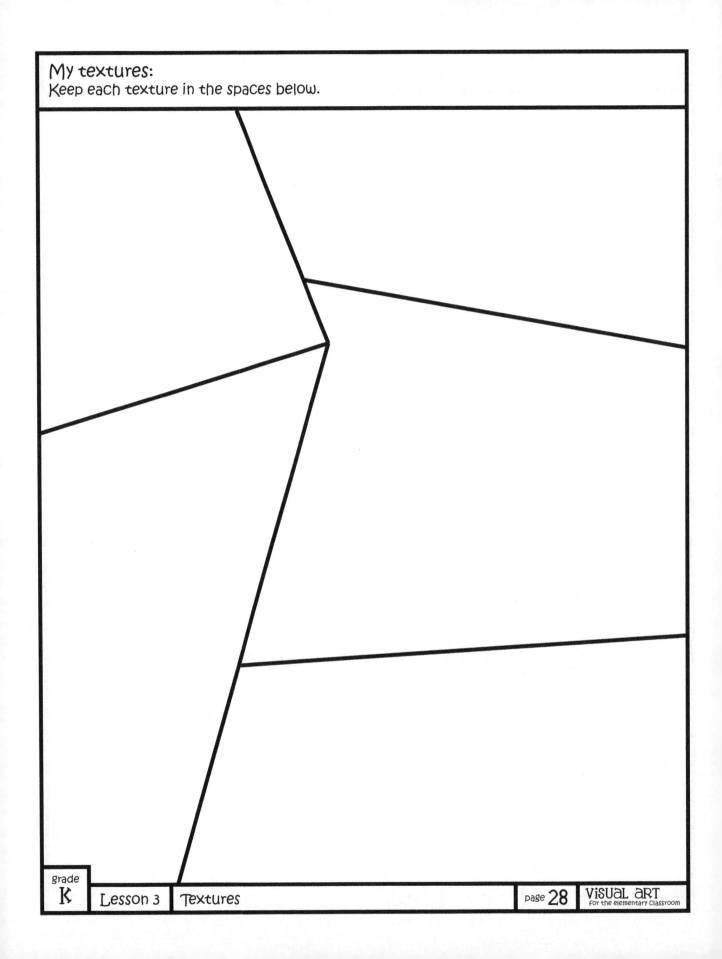

My Pattern:
Draw a pattern of circles, squares and triangles.

My Bug:

My Bug's Name: _____

Which bug (2D or 3D) I like better and why:

My Object:

My object's everyday use:

Our town's name: _____

My building:

My Person's Name: _____

My Person:

Student Name _____

Lesson	Participation	Completion	Art Journal	
LESSON 1 Color Basics	1 2 3 4 5 Total _____	1 2 3 4 5 (15)	1 2 3 4 5	_____ _____
LESSON 2 Shapes	1 2 3 4 5 Total _____	1 2 3 4 5 (15)	1 2 3 4 5	_____ _____
LESSON 3 Textures	1 2 3 4 5 Total _____	1 2 3 4 5 (15)	1 2 3 4 5	_____ _____
LESSON 4 Dancing Shapes	1 2 3 4 5 Total _____	1 2 3 4 5 (15)	1 2 3 4 5	_____ _____
LESSON 5 Bugs 2D	1 2 3 4 5 Total _____	1 2 3 4 5 (15)	1 2 3 4 5	_____ _____
LESSON 6 Bugs 3D	1 2 3 4 5 Total _____	1 2 3 4 5 (15)	1 2 3 4 5	_____ _____
LESSON 7 Everyday Objects	1 2 3 4 5 Total _____	1 2 3 4 5 (15)	1 2 3 4 5	_____ _____
LESSON 8 Our Town: Places	1 2 3 4 5 Total _____	1 2 3 4 5 (15)	1 2 3 4 5	_____ _____
LESSON 9 Our Town: People	1 2 3 4 5 Total _____	1 2 3 4 5 (15)	1 2 3 4 5	_____ _____

15 POINTS: UNIT TOTAL (135):

A = 13-15   A = 117-135
B = 11-12   B = 99-116
C = 9-10   C = 81-98
D = 8   D = 72-80

Participation: student's participation during the lesson.
Completion: student's work - did they follow directions, finish the assignment, show self-expression.
Art Journal: student work on lesson reflection pages.

The following pages are lesson plans for grade one. The lessons build off each other and include objectives, procedures and supplies needed. Art journals should consist of blank paper to draw/sketch and lesson reflecting pages.

Objectives:

Students will start to learn about color theory, and how to create secondary colors (combinations of red/yellow, yellow/blue and blue/red; orange, green and purple [violet]).

Procedures:

1. What are the primary colors?

2. What are the secondary colors? Who knows how to make secondary colors?

3. Demonstrate (with tempera) how to create secondary colors and instruct students that they will be mixing their own colors. First have students paint squares with primary colors. Then they mix equal amounts of two primary colors to create orange, green and purple squares.

4. Allow students to experiment with mixing 2 primary colors. What happens when they mix red and yellow, but with more red than yellow? etc.

5. Students cut shapes of their choice out of the dry colored squares, and glue them on black paper forming a color wheel.

6. Students reflect in their art journals, using the corresponding lesson reflecting page.

Supplies needed:

Art journal page, white paper squares of 4-5inches, tempera paints in only red, yellow and blue, brushes, black paper 9x12 or larger, glue, scissors, (crayons, pencils or markers for the art journal).

Objectives:
Students will use their knowledge of secondary colors to create a still life portrait using only secondary colors.

Procedures:

1. Review what the secondary colors are.

2. Give students oil pastels, having them choose only the secondary colors (variations of colors allowed) and black and white.

3. Place several common simple shaped objects for students all to see (apple, orange, cup, stuffed animal, etc) and tell students to draw these items, and color them using only the secondary colors. Colors do not need to match the color of the object, and can be student choice. But, the viewer should be able to identify what the object is.

4. Students share their creations and reflect in their art journals, using the corresponding lesson reflecting page.

Supplies needed:
Art journal page, white paper 9x12 or larger, oil pastels in only secondary colors plus black and white, (crayons, pencils or markers for the art journal).

Objectives:

Students will use clay to create an animal or other object that they view. They will use texture and color to represent the characteristics of the animal.

Procedures:

1. Give students photos of animals to view while creating their 3D still life. (Students don't need to have more than a couple options).

2. Discuss with students the rules of working with clay (no throwing, etc.), and have them put on aprons or other clothing to cover their clothes.

3. Place a large piece of paper for students to work on, protecting the table surface), and give each student some clay to work with. Allow them to work and play with it first before starting their animal.

4. Make sure the students have instruments to add texture to their pieces. (Toothpicks, tongue-depressers, etc).

5. After drying for 24 hours, allow students to use a choice of markers, tempera or watercolors to color their creations.

6. Students share their creations and reflect in their art journals, using the corresponding lesson reflecting page.

Supplies needed:

Art journal page, air-drying clay, paper to cover tables, aprons, instruments to add texture to the clay, markers, tempera and watercolors, animals to view/work from.

Objectives:

Students will learn about Victor Vasarely and his art, and create a piece of their own showing repetition.

Procedures:

1. Read aloud the summary about Victor Vasarely stopping and discussing the ideas of Vasarely and repetition.

2. Go over the guidelines for creating a pattern. Have students choose a 5 shape pattern using 3 different shapes (square, circle and triangle), drawing them on their art journal page.

3. Pass out a blank sheet of black (or white) paper and 2 inch squares of various colored paper. Students should glue the squares in a random pattern on the paper covering the whole sheet.

4. Students use white (or yellow) shapes (squares, circles and triangles) to recreate their chosen pattern on the colored squares. The pattern should go from left to right, then right to left, and so on.

5. Students share their creations and reflect in their art journals, using the corresponding lesson reflecting page.

Supplies needed:

Art journal page, Vasarely bio page, examples of his art (available at www.evisualart.com), black paper 12x12 or larger, 2 inch squares of blue, green, red, purple, brown, and orange paper, smaller than 2 inches squares, circles and triangles in white paper, glue.

victor vasarely

(1906-1997) Hungary

Born in Hungary, Victor Vasarely studied medicine before quitting to enter art school. During this time, he began creating abstract art. He left Hungary and went to Paris in 1938 where he was employed as a graphic artist for an advertising agency.

Vasarely was fascinated with linear and abstract patterns that created optical illusions. He used various colors and lightening/darkening of colors to form movement and flow in his art. He tried to create two-dimensional visual energy that was made by the placement of geometric shapes and controlling the colors he used.

Vasarely was connected to the Op Art (optical) movement and inspired young artists in Paris to explore ideas of graphical art similar to his.

Objectives:
Students will use their knowledge of repeating patterns to create a group pattern which they will present visually through clapping and movement.

Procedures:
1. Describe the project to the students. In groups, students will create a pattern using circles, triangles and squares. Decide on how many claps each shape represents (e.g., circle = 2, square = 3, square = 1).

2. Divide students into groups of 5.

3. They create their pattern, and practice before presenting it to the class. The groups draw the pattern on the board for all to see. Each group needs to repeat their pattern 5 times.

4. After all presentations, have students get into groups again, and this time they determine what the shapes of their pattern equal (e.g., a clap, a turn). They present these to the class also.

5. Students reflect in their art journals, using the corresponding lesson reflecting page.

Supplies needed:
Art journal page.

Objectives:
Students will learn about patterns they see in nature, and create a 3-dimensional spiral pattern of their own.

Procedures:
1. Discuss patterns that we see in nature. Go outside and view patterns around the school.
2. Show students samples of spiral patterns.
3. Discuss different types of textures, drawing them on the board. Students need to include different textures in their spiral.
4. Go over the rules of working with clay, put on protective aprons, place paper over the table surface and give each student some clay to work with. Allow them to work and play with it first before starting their spiral.
5. After drying, students color their spirals with markers, tempera or watercolors.
6. Students share their creations and reflect in their art journals, using the corresponding lesson reflecting page.

Supplies needed:
Art journal page, spiral examples (available at www.evisualart.com), air-drying clay, paper to cover tables, aprons, instruments to add texture to the clay, markers, tempera and watercolors.

Objectives:

Students will create a class-wide pattern, sort their creations into categories and discuss why people create art.

Procedures:

1. Why do we make art? Lead a discussion.

2. Instruct students as to the class-wide pattern that they are going to create. Each student will create 3 squares of the pattern.

3. Students will choose a background color square for each and then glue one of each shape on each. Students add texture and color each shape.

4. Students sort the squares first by shape.

5. Students then sort the squares by background color and/or texture.

6. Let them work together to create the pattern which is then displayed in the room.

Supplies needed:

6-9 inch squares (whatever you choose) of blue, green, orange, red, purple and brown paper, white circles, squares and triangles that are smaller than the colored squares, oil pastels to add texture, glue.

Objectives:

Students will create a piece that reflects on what they have learned about patterns, texture and shapes to create an abstract animal. They will describe why they create art, and what they like/dislike about creating art.

Procedures:

1. Students use their 3D animal as a guide to create their 2D animal portrait.

2. Students draw their animal first, and then add texture/patterns to it, using watercolors, oil pastels, tempera or markers, or a combination of media.

3. Students share their creations, describing the choices they made for their animal and why they create art. They will also reflect on their likes/dislikes in their art journals.

Supplies needed:

Art journal page, white paper 9x12 or larger, students' 3D animal, markers, oil pastels, tempera or watercolors.

The 3 Primary Colors are:

The 3 Secondary Colors are:

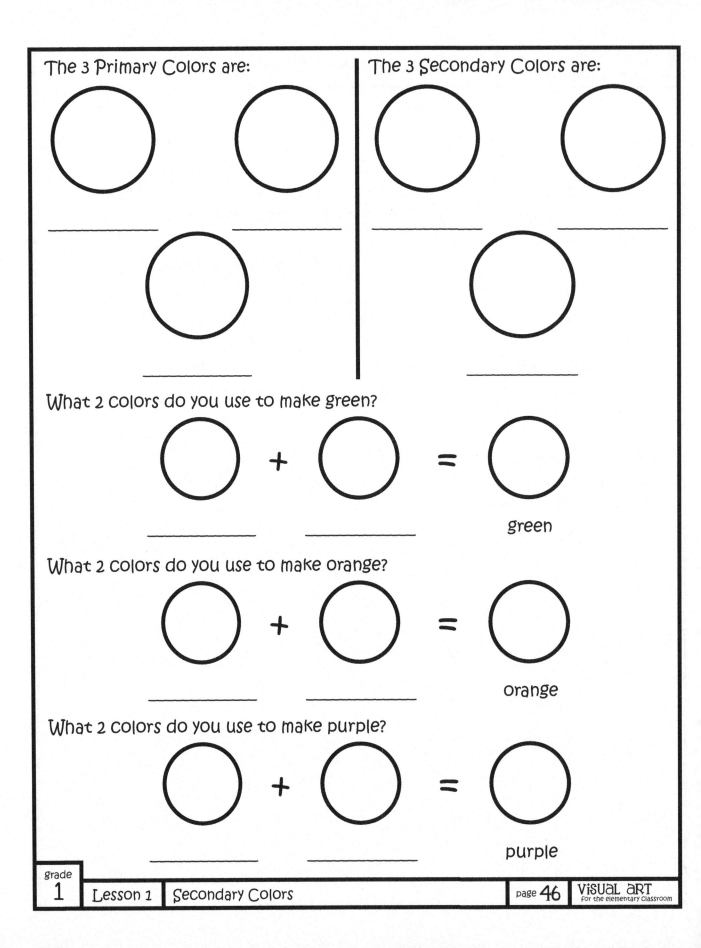

What 2 colors do you use to make green?

+ = green

What 2 colors do you use to make orange?

+ = orange

What 2 colors do you use to make purple?

+ = purple

What I like about my art:

_____

— —

_____

— —

_____

— —

_____

What I would change about my art:

_____

— —

_____

_____

— —

_____

— —

_____

Why I made my animal:

_____

— — — — — — — — — — — — — — — — — —

_____

— — — — — — — — — — — — — — — — — —

_____

— — — — — — — — — — — — — — — — — —

_____

What I used to make my animal:

_____

— — — — — — — — — — — — — — — — — —

_____

_____

— — — — — — — — — — — — — — — — — —

_____

_____

— — — — — — — — — — — — — — — — — —

_____

My pattern: (using only Circles, triangles and squares)

The colors I used in my art pattern:

What I like about my pattern/picture:

_____

- -

_____

_____

- -

_____

_____

- -

_____

◯ = _____
Clap(s)

△ = _____
Clap(s)

▢ = _____
Clap(s)

Our pattern: (using only circles, triangles and squares)

◯ = _____

△ = _____

▢ = _____

Our second pattern: (using only circles, triangles and squares)

Practice spiral:

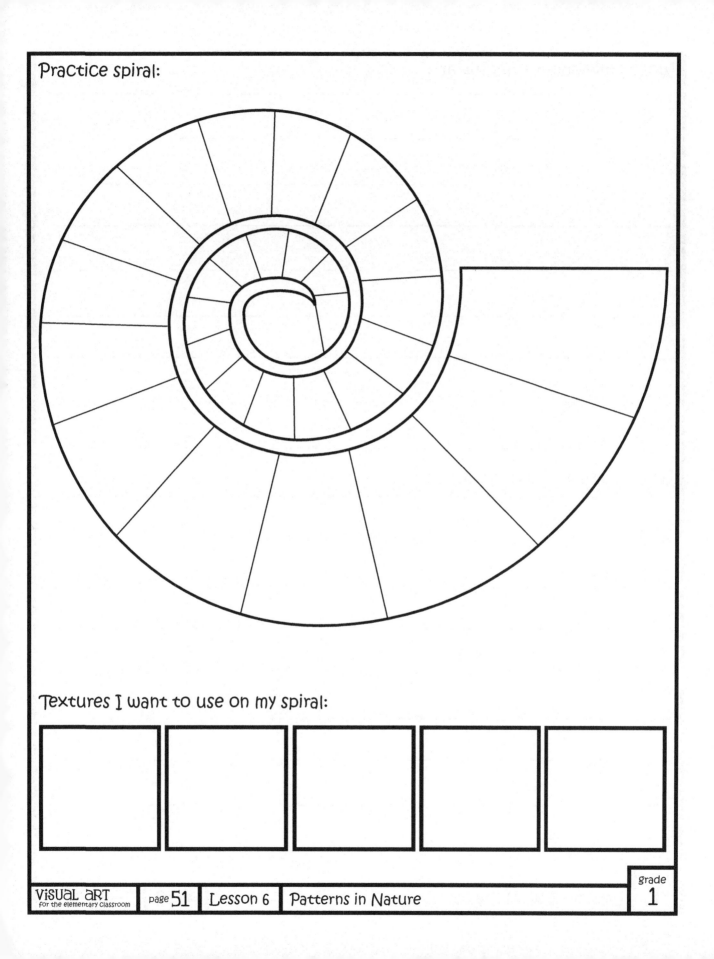

Textures I want to use on my spiral:

What I like about Creating art:

_____

– –

_____

– –

_____

– –

_____

What I dislike about Creating art:

_____

– –

_____

– –

_____

– –

_____

Student Name _____

Lesson	Participation	Completion	Art Journal	
LESSON 1 Secondary Colors	1 2 3 4 5 Total _____	1 2 3 4 5 (15)	1 2 3 4 5	_____ _____
LESSON 2 Secondary Still Life	1 2 3 4 5 Total _____	1 2 3 4 5 (15)	1 2 3 4 5	_____ _____
LESSON 3 Still Life 3D	1 2 3 4 5 Total _____	1 2 3 4 5 (15)	1 2 3 4 5	_____ _____
LESSON 4 Vasarely Repetition	1 2 3 4 5 Total _____	1 2 3 4 5 (15)	1 2 3 4 5	_____ _____
LESSON 5 Rhythmic Patterns	1 2 3 4 5 Total _____	1 2 3 4 5 (20)	1 2 3 4 5	Group work: 1 2 3 4 5 _____
LESSON 6 Patterns in Nature	1 2 3 4 5 Total _____	1 2 3 4 5 (15)	1 2 3 4 5	_____ _____
LESSON 7 Why We Create Art	1 2 3 4 5 Total _____	1 2 3 4 5 (15)	Class work: 1 2 3 4 5	_____ _____
LESSON 8 Why I Create Art	1 2 3 4 5 Presentation: 1 2 3 4 5 Total _____	1 2 3 4 5 6 7 8 9 10 (25)	Art Journal: 1 2 3 4 5	_____ _____

15 POINTS:	20 POINTS:	25 POINTS:	UNIT TOTAL (135):
A = 13-15	A = 18-20	A = 22-25	A = 118-135
B = 11-12	B = 16-17	B = 19-21	B = 101-117
C = 9-10	C = 14-15	C = 16-18	C = 84-100
D = 8	D = 12-13	D = 12-13	D = 73-83

Participation: student's participation during the lesson.
Completion: student's work - did they follow directions, finish the assignment, show self-expression.
Art Journal: student work on lesson reflection pages.

The following pages are lesson plans for grade two. The lessons build off each other and include objectives, procedures and supplies needed.

Objectives:
Students will learn about warm colors and create a warm landscape collage.

Procedures:
1. What are the warm colors? (reds through yellows, including browns and tans) Discuss and write on the board.

2. What objects in nature are warm colors? (sun, fire, etc)

3. What season is associated? Moods?

4. Make sure all the objects and associations to warm colors are written for all to see, and used to create their art.

5. Students plan out their work first in their art journal, determining what landscape they are going to do, objects in it, etc.

6. Give students warm color tissue paper and construction paper to use in their piece.

7. Students that finish early can write a reflection of what they know about warm colors and how warm colors make them feel.

8. Share art and mood created in their art.

Supplies needed:
Art journal, white paper 9x12 or larger, tissue and construction paper in warm colors, glue, scissors.

Objectives:
Students will learn about cool colors and create a cool landscape.

Procedures:

1. What are the cool colors? (blue-green through violet, including greys) Discuss and write on the board.

2. What objects in nature are warm colors? (water, snow, sky, clouds, etc)

3. What season is associated? Moods?

4. Make sure all the objects and associations to cool colors are written for all to see, and used to create their art.

5. Students plan out their work first in their art journal, determining what landscape they are going to do, objects in it, etc.

6. Give students oil pastels, having them use only the cool colors.

7. Students that finish early can write a reflection of what they know about cool colors and how cool colors make them feel.

8. Share art and mood created in their art.

Supplies needed:
Art journal, white paper 9x12 or larger, oil pastels - using only the cool colors.

Objectives:

Students will create a warm or cool landscaped based on their previous warm or cool creation. They will compare the two images, the mood they both create and place them into categories based on the moods.

Procedures:

1. Students choose either their warm landscape or cool landscape.

2. Students use this landscape to create an opposite version of it. They can use collage, watercolors, tempera or oil pastels to create their work.

3. Share the warm vs. cool versions, discussing the moods they create and why, and group them into categories based on those moods.

4. Students reflect on their work in their art journals.

Supplies needed:

Previous warm/cool landscapes from lessons 1 and 2, paper for collage, oil pastels, watercolors, tempera, glue, scissors.

Objectives:

Students will learn about bilateral and radial symmetry, finding examples in the classroom and nature, and create a butterfly collage.

Procedures:

1. Lead a discussion on bilateral and radial symmetry. Show students images of both. (Bilateral = on one plane, a mirror image on both sides, Radial = on multiple planes, mirroring images)

2. Ask students to find other objects with bilateral symmetry (radial may be hard to find since it is mostly found in sea organisms).

3. Students share items and show why it has symmetry.

4. Demonstrate how to draw and cut out a butterfly. Fold a paper in half and draw half a butterfly body. And then do the same for its wings.

5. Students do the same, and then use colored paper to create shapes to put on their butterfly, making sure that they are placed in the same position on both wings.

6. If students finish early, let them create leaves by folding paper and cutting them out.

7. Create a space for all the butterflies and leaves to be displayed together.

Supplies needed:

Sample symmetry examples (available at www.evisualart.com), colored paper for the butterflies and leaves (brown, red, orange or purple for the body; black or other colors for the wings; green for the leaves), glue, scissors.

Objectives:

Students will learn about Jasper Johns, his work, identify and define vocabulary and work in small groups to create a Johns style art piece.

Procedures:

1. Read aloud the summary about Jasper Johns, stopping and discussing the ideas of Johns, and identifying vocabulary.

2. View several works by Johns and ask students about their thoughts and feelings regarding Johns and his art.

3. Divide students into groups of 4-5 and discuss guidelines for creating their piece. They can only use primary colors plus black, white and greys and basic shapes (stars, circles, triangles, squares, lines) and numbers and letters.

4. Students choose up to 3 basic shapes, and several numbers or letters.

5. Make sure students plan out their work, sketching it first. They should repeat the objects, increase or decrease sizing and colors to depict the illusion of space in their work.

6. Students work together using the media of their choosing.

7. Students share their finished pieces.

Supplies needed:

Johns handout, samples of Johns art (available at www.evisualart.com), white paper 9x12 or larger, mixed media of the students' choice.

JASPER JOHNS

(1930-present) Augusta, Georgia

Jasper Johns was born in Georgia, but grew up in South Carolina. He moved to New York at the age of 22 and became friends with other artists living there. Throughout his career, Johns painted images and objects from popular culture because they were from what the mind already knows. He is associated with the Pop Art movement because of this.

In his early art, he started using wax-based paints that dry quickly. This enabled him to create distinctive brush strokes rapidly and without the usual wait for paint to dry. Johns used white, black, grey and the three primary colors to create his art.

In the 1960s Jasper Johns turned to printmaking as his primary technique, which led to innovations in silk-screening, lithography and etching.

His works have been sold for millions of dollars, and his large paintings are popular among collectors because they are very rare.

Objectives:

Students will use their knowledge of Jasper Johns, repetition and objects in nature that have symmetry to create a new Johns/nature piece.

Procedures:

1. Discuss what the students know about Jasper Johns, and objects in nature with symmetry.

2. Divide students into the same groups as in the previous lesson.

3. Instruct students to use their Johns piece from before as a guide for their new piece. They need to replace all objects that are not symmetrical with objects in nature that are (leaves, bugs, etc.). They use any media again to create their new piece.

4. Students share the new work, comparing it to their previous work, describing the differences.

Supplies needed:

Previous Jasper Johns group art, white paper 9x12 or larger, mixed media of the students' choice.

Objectives:

Students will learn about Andy Warhol, his work, identify and define vocabulary and create their own self portrait.

Procedures:

NOTE: Before beginning this lesson, take photos of students to create their self-portrait. This should be from the shoulders up and students can pose or just stare at the camera. Print out photos to fit on letter size paper. Use the copier to adjust the contrast to create black and white print (no greys). Print each portrait on art paper or watercolor paper, (make 3 copies of each, 2 to use in the next lesson).

1. Read aloud the summary about Andy Warhol, stopping and discussing the ideas of Warhol, and identifying vocabulary.

2. View several works by Warhol and ask students about their thoughts and feelings regarding Warhol, his art and PopArt.

3. Students choose any 3 colors and write them down. Each student will use those colors on their portrait.

4. Pass out the copied black and white portrait. Students use watercolors to color their portrait in an Andy Warhol style.

5. Share student work and have students reflect in their journals.

Supplies needed:

Warhol handout, samples of Warhol art (available at www.evisualart.com), art journal, watercolors, brushes, camera, art/watercolor paper cut to fit into copier.

(Students can create hero portraits if you choose to align more with the California visual art standard 5.2 and create a hero report.)

ANDY WARHOL
(1928-1987) Pennsylvania

It is not sure when Andy Warhol was born, because he said he was born in 1928 and his birth certificate proved to be a forgery. He was born Andrew Warhola, but changed it to Warhol after moving to New York in 1949. Warhol loved to be mysterious and sometimes had a look-a-like impersonate him in the public.

He was a very public figure and attended many parties and public events. Warhol socialized with many famous people and had many workers in his art studio which he called "The Factory". Although he was primarily an artist, he was also a film-maker and businessman. He believed that "art gained beauty primarily through money."

Andy Warhol also coined the phrase "famous for 15 minutes".

In his art, Warhol used iconic American products such as the Campbell's Soup can and bottles of Coca-Cola, and celebrities of his time, like Marilyn Monroe, Elvis Presley, Troy Donahue, Muhammad Ali and Elizabeth Taylor. One of his works of Elvis sold for $100 million.

Objectives:
Students will use expressive warm and cool colors to create warm and cool self portraits and then discuss their portraits.

Procedures:

1. Discuss prior knowledge of warm and cool colors and Andy Warhol.

2. Students create warm portraits and cool portraits using their copied black and white portraits and watercolors.

3. Share the portraits with the class, discussing the mood created by both. Compare also with their portraits from the last lesson. Which portrait shows their personality? Why did they use those colors? Do they like/dislike what they have created? Have students group their findings into the different categories.

4. Students can reflect on their works in their art journals.

Supplies needed:
Art journal, watercolors, brushes, copied portraits on art/watercolor paper.

Objectives:
Students will learn about Andy Warhol's camouflage and how it differs from ordinary camouflage (stands out instead of blending in). They will create their own camouflage color combinations, expressing moods.

Procedures:

1. Discuss how colors express moods or themes. Write down answers for all students to see and use.

2. Students choose a mood and 4 colors to express that mood.

3. View Andy Warhol's Camouflage Suite and read about his camouflage and discuss how it is different from ordinary camouflage and any feelings they create.

4. Pass out blank camouflage sheets and allow students to only use the four colors they choose.

5. After students have colored their camouflage, cut them out and after discussing them and their intended/perceived moods. (Display them together, creating a colorful camouflage quilt.)

Supplies needed:
Warhol Camouflage handout, "Camouflage Suite" art (available at www.evisualart. com), camouflage coloring sheet, markers or oil pastels.

ANDY WARHOL CAMOUFLAGE

Camouflage is designed by artists at a military's request and it first started to be used in the early 20th century. Camouflage was used for the concealment of equipment, and then on service worker uniforms.

Unlike the military's, Warhol's camouflages show bright, inorganic colors which would stand out instead of hide in a landscape. Camouflage also gave him the opportunity to work with a recognizable image and an abstract pattern. As Warhol created more camouflages, he began to place them into his self-portraits.

Camouflage?   Name_____

my colors: 1 = [____]   2 = [____]   3 = [____]   4 = [____]

Objectives:

Students will reflect on what they have learned during the previous art lessons. They will use this knowledge to create a piece of their choice which expresses an aspect of what they have learned.

Procedures:

1. Discuss what the students have learned in the previous lessons (warm, cool colors, symmetry, about Jasper Johns and Andy Warhol, moods, themes).

2. Students create a reflective piece that uses one aspect of what they have learned or more.

3. Students share their creations.

Supplies needed:

Students use media of their choice.

Student Name _____

Lesson	Participation	Completion	Art Journal	
LESSON 1￼Warm Colors	1 2 3 4 5￼Total _____	1 2 3 4 5￼(15)	1 2 3 4 5	_____￼_____
LESSON 2￼Cool Colors	1 2 3 4 5￼Total _____	1 2 3 4 5￼(15)	1 2 3 4 5	_____￼_____
LESSON 3￼Warm vs. Cool	1 2 3 4 5￼Total _____	1 2 3 4 5￼(10)		_____￼_____
LESSON 4￼Found in Nature	1 2 3 4 5￼Total _____	1 2 3 4 5￼(10)		_____￼_____
LESSON 5￼Jasper Johns	1 2 3 4 5￼Total _____	1 2 3 4 5￼(15)	Group work: 1 2 3 4 5	_____￼_____
LESSON 6￼Repetition with Nature	1 2 3 4 5￼Total _____	1 2 3 4 5￼(15)	Group work: 1 2 3 4 5	_____￼_____
LESSON 7￼Andy Warhol	1 2 3 4 5￼Total _____	1 2 3 4 5￼(15)	1 2 3 4 5	_____￼_____
LESSON 8￼Warhol Warm and Cool	1 2 3 4 5￼Total _____	1 2 3 4 5￼(15)	Warm & Cool usage: 1 2 3 4 5	_____￼_____
LESSON 9￼Camouflage?	1 2 3 4 5￼Total _____	1 2 3 4 5￼(25)		_____￼_____
LESSON 10￼What I know	Participation:￼Completion:￼Total _____	1 2 3 4 5 6 7 8 9 10￼1 2 3 4 5 6 7 8 9 10￼(20)		_____￼_____￼_____

10 POINTS:	15 POINTS:	20 POINTS:	UNIT TOTAL (140):
A = 9-10	A = 13-15	A = 18-20	A = 123-140
B = 7-8	B = 11-12	B = 16-17	B = 103-122
C = 6	C = 9-10	C = 14-15	C = 86-102
D = 5	D = 8	D = 12-13	D = 75-85

Participation: student's participation during the lesson.
Completion: student's work - did they follow directions, finish the assignment, show self-expression.
Art Journal: student has written about the lesson.

The following pages are lesson plans for grade three. The lessons build off each other and include objectives, procedures and supplies needed.

Objectives:
Students will learn about Piet Mondrian, his work, identify and define vocabulary and create their own Mondrian style art.

Procedures:

1. Read aloud the summary about Piet Mondrian, stopping and discussing the ideas of Mondrian, and identifying vocabulary and writing their definitions in student art journals.

2. View several works by Mondrian and ask students about their thoughts and feelings regarding Mondrian and his art.

3. Write guidelines for the students to create their own Mondrian style work. (Only use red, blue and yellow and black, white and grey, and horizontal and vertical lines.)

4. Students draw straight vertical and horizontal lines on their white paper, and then decide what colors to use and where.

5. Once students have painted the areas with solid color (and they are dry) use black strips of paper or black tape to create the black lines.

6. Make sure all students write a reflection about Mondrian and their art in their art journal.

Supplies needed:
Mondrian handout, samples of Mondrian art (available at www.evisualart.com), art journal, white paper 9x12 or larger, red, blue and yellow tempera paints, paint brushes, black strips of paper or black tape.

PIET MONDRIAN

(1872-1944) Holland

Piet Mondrian started as a landscape painter, but by 1906 he was beginning to turn his landscapes into flat geometric patterns. He believed that all paintings are made of lines and colors, and broke down aspects of nature into simple geometric shapes. Mondrian wanted to create balance and perfection in his art.

His main ideas that all art should try to adhere to are:

1. All paintings are composed of line and color.

2. Paintings must be as flat as the surface it is painted on.

3. The simpler the form, the more nearly it is universal. Hence, the simplest form of all, the rectangle, must constitute the sole form if painting is to achieve university.

4. The only pure colors are the primary ones... Hence they alone may be used, each pure in itself.[1]

Mondrian only used primary colors, (red, yellow, blue), primary values, (white, black, grey), and primary directions, (vertical, horizontal).

[1] ideas 1-4 are directly quoted from Mainstreams in Modern Art, 1981, by John Canaday.

Objectives:

Students will define the terms, tints, shades and neutral colors. They will create tints and shades of red, yellow or blue, practicing their color mixing. Students will expand on their first Mondrian art by creating a new version containing tints, shades and neutrals.

Procedures:

1. Ask questions like: How would Mondrian's work be different if he used tints, shades and neutral colors? Write answers on the board.

2. Define tint, shade and neutral colors.
   (tint: mixing a color with white.)
   (shade: mixing a color with black.)
   (neutral colors: greys ranging from black to white. Greys can include warm and cool greys, which include small parts of other colors.)

3. Students create strips of red, yellow or blue tints and shades (1 of each, tint and shade). They can also create mixes of black with white to create greys.

4. Using their first Mondrian piece as a guide, students create their new work, painting with tints, shades and neutrals.

5. Choose several student pieces to compare and share.

6. Students write in their art journal comparing their two works, and how they feel Mondrian's art would be if he used tints, shades and neutrals.

Supplies needed:

Art journal, white paper strips 4x12, white paper 9x12 or larger, red, blue, yellow, black and white tempera paints, paint brushes, black strips of paper or black tape.

Objectives:
Students will learn about Georges Seurat and his art. They will identify and define foreground, middle ground, background, and secondary colors (green, orange, purple).

Procedures:
1. Read aloud the summary about Seurat, stopping to answer and ask questions.

2. View several works by Seurat, having students find shapes, directions and colors in the works, and how these elements represent foreground, middle ground and background. Define these terms.

3. Define secondary colors.

4. Display several ordinary objects for students to work from.

5. Pass out white paper and have students draw the basic shapes they see in the object(s) displayed.

6. Demonstrate how to apply "dots" to paper, creating a Seurat-like piece. (Pre-punch dots of varying colors for students to use, or if time, allow students to punch their own.)

7. Students glue their dots, creating their art.

8. Share art and discuss and compare their art.

9. Students reflect about Seurat and their work in their art journal.

Supplies needed:
Seurat summary, samples of Seurat's work (available at www.evisualart.com), art journal, white paper 9x12 or larger, punched dots of varying colors, glue, common objects.

Georges Seurat

(1859-91) France

Georges Seurat lived a short life, only 32 years, but he created major contributions to the art world. He began as an Impressionist painter (one who represents the visual character of subjects or landscapes without recreating reality).

Seurat took Impressionism a step further, adding a scientific approach to his art. He created his art with dots of primary and secondary colors, making the viewer's eyes mix them into more complex colors. Up close, the viewer sees only the dots of color, and as they move farther away, the colors mix, creating the complex colors and shapes. Seurat also emphasized horizontal and vertical lines to create depth and movement, but keeping a formal approach to his work. He painted shapes that formed representations of his subjects, using also flat patterns.

Objectives:

Students will compare and contrast the works of Mondrian and Seurat.

Procedures:

1. Ask questions like: What do we know about Mondrian? What do we know about Seurat? Write down student answers. Discuss how they are similar and different. Show works by both to refresh and compare.

2. Students review their Mondrian and Seurat art also.

3. Students write about their views on Mondrian's and Seurat's art, comparing and contrasting the two painters. Make sure they use their art journal reflections and art terms in their writing.

4. Discuss and share student writings.

5. Students that finish their writing early may sketch in their art journals.

Supplies needed:

Art journals, samples of Mondrian and Seurat work.

Objectives:
Students will use their prior knowledge of tints, shades, neutrals, primary colors, secondary colors, foreground, middle ground, and background to create art that has the illusion of space. Students will create a poem or story about their space-scape.

Procedures:

1. Review prior knowledge of tints, shades, foreground, middle ground and background, and how these art elements create the illusion of space.

2. Students sketch their ideas for creating their own cityscape, landscape or seascape. Their painting must have a repetition of elements/shapes (like buildings or trees), and use tints and shades of colors to create the illusion of space. (Elements in front should be brighter and larger than the rest.) Their scape should be made-up and not an actual place.

3. Students name their scape and describe it in their art journal, explaining how they created their space-scape.

4. Students either write a short poem or story about what happens in their space-scape.

Supplies needed:
Art journals, white paper 9x12 or larger, tempera paints, paint brushes, lined paper for poem or story.

Objectives:
Students will discover and identify what are warm and cool colors and the illusion of depth they create.

Procedures:

1. Tell students that there are warm colors and cool colors, and ask them to identify a warm and a cool color and why they think that their chosen colors are warm and cool.

2. Give students (or have them make) large (5-6 in) and small (1-2 in) squares of red, yellow, orange, green, blue and purple.

3. Students experiment with placing a small cool color on top of a large warm color and vice versa. Does one color look closer or further away than the other?

4. Discuss student thoughts and have them glue several combinations together with a sentence or two describing which is closer or further.

5. Students reflect on their findings in their art journals.

Supplies needed:
Art journals, white paper 9x12 or larger, colored 5-6 inch and 1-2 inch squares of red, yellow, orange, green, blue, and purple, glue.

Objectives:

Students will learn about Paul Cezanne and his art. They will describe and identify warm and cool colors, and use this knowledge to create a scene from life that has rhythm and movement.

Procedures:

1. Read aloud the summary about Paul Cezanne, stopping and discussing along the way.

2. View several works by Cezanne, describing his color use of warm colors in the foreground and cool colors in the background.

3. Take students outside, or bring them photos of the area where they live to work from.

4. On white paper, students draw their scene and decide on the colors they want to use and where.

5. Students paint or use pastels to create their scene.

6. Students reflect on Cezanne and the use of warm and cool colors to create depth.

7. Share student art.

Supplies needed:

Cezanne summary, samples of his work (available at www.evisualart.com), art journals, white paper 9x12 or larger, tempera paints, paint brushes, or oil pastels.

PAUL CEZANNE

(1839-1906) France

Color and the structure that color creates was the focus of Paul Cezanne. He aimed to not create realistic or photographic art with his paintings. Color was the most important art element for Cezanne. He believed that color dictates space, depth, shapes, light and dark, and distances.

Cezanne developed planes of color in his art. Warm colors to the front, and cool colors in the back. The combination and use of warm and cool colors indicate depth in his work.

Cezanne also distorted shapes to portray expression. Accurate perspective was not his goal, as the subject of his art was not as important as his representation through use of colors and shapes.

Objectives:
Students will view the work - The House with Burst Walls - by Cezanne and describe, in a story and picture, what they think will happen next in the scene.

Procedures:

1. Show students the work by Cezanne and leave it up for students to view.

2. Ask students to think about what they think will happen next in the scene, and write some notes in their art journals.

3. Pair up the students, and have them work together to create a story and a picture of what will happen next. Each person must work on both the writing and picture. Students use their knowledge of art elements to create their art.

4. Mount art and story together and have students tell their stories.

Supplies needed:
Art journals, white paper about 9x12, tempera paints, paint brushes, oil pastels, lined paper for story, colored paper to mount story and picture, glue.

Objectives:
Students will reflect on their art knowledge to identify and describe why art is important and what are art elements that make art represent life, objects and scenes. Students will work together to present their findings.

Procedures:

1. Discuss and write students knowledge of art, artists, and art elements. Students can refer to their art journals.

2. Divide students into groups of 4-5 and have them work together to create a brief report on art. Their report can include: tints and shapes, illusions of space, elements of art. Their report should include: what they have learned about either, Mondrian, Seurat or Cezanne and what makes their art successful and how they feel about the artists and their art.

3. Students present their reports to the rest of the class and can even include drawings or art they have produced.

Supplies needed:
Art journals, lined paper, information on artist.

Objectives:
Students will use their art knowledge to create a collage of art elements that draw on what they have learned about Mondrian, Seurat and Cezanne.

Procedures:

1. Review the art elements each artist used in their work. Mondrian - primary lines and colors, Seurat - dots of primary and secondary colors, Cezanne - planes of warm and cool colors.

2. Ask students to think of a scene they want to create and sketch it in their art journals, identifying areas where they use techniques of the artists.

3. Students draw and compose their art.

4. Share art creations.

Supplies needed:
Art journals, white paper 9x12 or larger, tempera paints, paint brushes, oil pastels.

Student Name _____

Lesson	Participation	Completion	Art Journal	
LESSON 1 Primary Mondrian	1 2 3 4 5 Total _____ (15)	1 2 3 4 5	1 2 3 4 5	_____ _____
LESSON 2 Tints, Shades and Neutrals	1 2 3 4 5 Total _____ (15)	1 2 3 4 5	1 2 3 4 5	_____ _____
LESSON 3 Seurat Dots	1 2 3 4 5 Total _____ (15)	1 2 3 4 5	1 2 3 4 5	_____ _____
LESSON 4 Mondrian vs. Seurat	1 2 3 4 5 Total _____ (10)	1 2 3 4 5		_____ _____
LESSON 5 Illusions of Space Scapes	1 2 3 4 5 Total _____ (20)	1 2 3 4 5	1 2 3 4 5	Poem/story: 1 2 3 4 5
LESSON 6 Warm and Cool	1 2 3 4 5 Total _____ (15)	1 2 3 4 5	1 2 3 4 5	_____ _____
LESSON 7 Cezanne	1 2 3 4 5 Total _____ (15)	1 2 3 4 5	1 2 3 4 5	_____ _____
LESSON 8 What Happens Next?	1 2 3 4 5 Total _____ (15)	1 2 3 4 5	Story/picture: 1 2 3 4 5	_____
LESSON 9 Why is Art Important?	1 2 3 4 5 6 7 8 9 10 Total _____ (25)	Report includes art elements, what student has learned, what makes successful art, student's feelings: 1 2 3 4 5 6 7 8 9 10 11 12 13 14 15		_____
LESSON 10 What I Know	1 2 3 4 5 Total _____ (10)	1 2 3 4 5		_____ _____

10 POINTS:	15 POINTS:	20 POINTS:	25 POINTS:	UNIT TOTAL (155):
A = 9-10	A = 13-15	A = 18-20	A = 22-25	A = 136-155
B = 7-8	B = 11-12	B = 16-17	B = 19-21	B = 115-135
C = 6	C = 9-10	C = 14-15	C = 16-18	C = 96-114
D = 5	D = 8	D = 12-13	D = 13-15	D = 83-95

Participation: student's participation during the lesson.
Completion: student's work - did they follow directions, finish the assignment, show self-expression.
Art Journal: student has written about the lesson.

The following pages are lesson plans for grade four. The lessons build off each other and include objectives, procedures and supplies needed.

Objectives:
Students will create color wheels, identify primary, secondary and complementary colors.

Procedures:

1. Ask students about color. What are primary and secondary colors? List them on the board.

2. Show students a large square of red and have them stare at it for 30 seconds, and then at a blank white area. What color do they see? They should see the complementary color of red. Try with blue and yellow.

3. Students draw a circle in their art journal, and divide it into six parts. They will then identify where the colors should be placed on their wheel.

4. Direct students to draw lines from the red to green, yellow to purple, blue to orange. These are complementary colors.

5. Give students blank paper and instruct them to paint areas of red, yellow, blue, green, orange and purple. Once dry, students will cut out shapes of their choosing and place them in a circle, creating their own color wheel. They should have enough color to also show the complementary pairs.

Supplies needed:
Art journals, white paper 9x12 or larger, tempera paints, paint brushes, scissors, glue, large squares of red, yellow and blue.

Objectives:

Students will learn about how complementary colors react when mixed together.

Procedures:

1. Review what complementary colors are.

2. Ask students what do they think will happen if they mix complementary colors together, writing their answers on the board.

3. Students work in groups of 3. Each student will mix a separate complementary pair.

4. Students will paint 5 squares of color mixes. (Example: One square green and one square red. Then they will mix a little of green with mostly red, and paint that on another square. They repeat the process with a little red with mostly green. For their last square, they mix half green and half red and paint that on their remaining square.)

5. While the paint drys, have students write in their art journal about the results of their mixes.

6. The groups glue their complementary pair mixes on one piece of paper, and include a brief summary of their results.

7. Share experiences, results and final works.

Supplies needed:

Art journals, 3 inch squares of white paper, white paper 9x12 or larger, lined paper, tempera paints, paint brushes, scissors, glue.

Objectives:

Students will learn about Vincent van Gogh and his paintings. They will identify the colors in his work and how they communicate mood. Students will describe and analyze art elements and use complementary and contrasting colors to create expression in their work.

Procedures:

1. Read aloud the summary about Van Gogh, stopping to answer and ask questions.

2. View several works by Van Gogh, and discuss the movement and color choices and the mood they create. View "Starry Night" last.

3. While viewing "Starry Night", have students write down their feelings. Review students answers, writing them down.

4. Go over different types of moods (stormy, dark, sunny, cold, hot, etc) and colors associated with each, listing them on the board.

5. Students sketch in their art journal a landscape and choose a mood they want to portray.

6. Give students white paper to paint on. Make sure they use the colors that represent their chosen mood, and they also use complementary, contrasting colors.

7. Share landscapes, having students guess the mood created.

8. Students reflect on Van Gogh, expression with color and texture, etc.

Supplies needed:

Van Gogh summary, samples of his work (available at www.evisualart.com), art journals, white paper 9x12 or larger, tempera paints, paint brushes.

VINCENT VAN GOGH

(1853-1890) Holland

The son of a pastor, Vincent van Gogh thought that he had a calling to do missionary work. As a result of many failures in school and relationships, Van Gogh finally started painting at age 27. His works were based on an expression of color and emotions. Unlike the scientific, flat dots that Georges Seurat regularly used in his paintings, Van Gogh created texture and movement through his brush strokes. He even was known to squeeze the paint directly from his paint tubes.

Early in his career, Van Gogh used gloomy colors that expressed city life around him. Later in his life, he turned to bright, bold colors that many painters of his day were using.

Van Gogh always experienced turmoil in his life, and in a strange incident, he cut off one of his ears. He suffered from seizures and hallucinations and even was in an asylum for a year. In 1890, Van Gogh shot himself below his heart and died two days later.

Objectives:

Students will learn about Henri Matisse and his art. They will also learn about and identify positive and negative space. Students will use contrasting color combinations to create art made of 2-dimensional, positive and negative shapes.

Procedures:

1. Read aloud the summary about Matisse, stopping to answer and ask questions.

2. View several works by Matisse, and discuss his color choices. Describe the use of positive and negative space and how it creates contrast in his work.

3. Cut construction paper to 9" x 6" or similar size. One color is the top and one is the bottom sheet. Distribute two sheets of the bottom sheet and the contrasting color for the one top sheet to each student. Make sure the colors are of contrasting colors (i.e. - red/green, blue/orange, yellow/purple, or blue/red, red/yellow, etc.)

4. Fold the top sheet in half along the 9" side, students then draw and carefully cut out half of a picture, design or several shapes/objects along the 9" length. The parts cut from the top sheet are arranged on one of the bottom sheets, creating half the design. The remaining parts are placed on the other bottom sheet in locations opposite those from which they were cut. Glue the parts down.

5. Glue the two finished sheets on a black or white piece of paper. The final project will have a positive image on one side and a negative image on the other.

6. Share the 2D art.

Supplies needed:

Matisse summary, samples of his work (available at www.evisualart.com), samples of pos/neg art, art journals, colored construction paper, scissors, glue.

HENRI MATISSE

(1869-1954) France

Originally trained as a lawyer, Henri Matisse first designed tapestry and textiles before becoming a painter. He studied many styles of painting before developing his own.

Matisse used bold color in unexpected ways in his art. He liked to have his pure colors clash against each other, creating a movement of color and movement between the colors. These colors were not blended, just placed next to each other, and did not necessarily represent the actual color of an object. A tree did not have to be a brown trunk with green leaves, it could be any color of Matisse's choosing. Color was more important than a true representation of the subject matter. Matisse wanted his paintings to evoke emotion through his color use.

Objectives:
Students will create 3-dimensional shapes by using shading techniques and positive and negative space.

Procedures:

1. Review knowledge of positive and negative space, 2-D shapes, and tints, shades and color values, defining each.

2. Show students how to create a 3-D object by altering the shade, tint and/or value.

3. Using their Matisse art as a reference, have students recreate the 2-D work into a 3-D art piece by using shading techniques. Positive and negative space is still important and should be considered in their work.

4. Share art, comparing the flat, 2-D to the 3-D.

5. Students reflect on the process of creating 3-D art in their art journals.

Supplies needed:
Art journals, white paper 9x12 or larger, oil pastels, art from Matisse lesson.

Objectives:

Students will learn to use facial proportions to create expressive portraits.

Procedures:

1. Demonstrate how to draw the human face, following these steps: (students can follow along, drawing in their art journals.) You may want to practice before demonstrating. Instructions can be written for all to reference.

    a. Fold a paper in half, creating two equal sections.
       (a 9x12 paper when folded would be 9x6)
    b. With a pencil, draw a large oval covering most of the paper.
    c. Divide the bottom half into thirds, by folding the paper or measuring.
    d. Fold or draw a line down the center (length) of the paper.
    e. Draw two eyes resting on the center line, leaving space in the middle for the nose.
    f. The tip (bottom) of the nose should be drawn on the second line.
    g. The mouth is placed slightly below the tip of the nose and the edges of the mouth should line up with the middle of the eyes.
    h. Begin the hairline about half way up the top half of the face.
    i. These steps show the correct proportions of creating a face.

2. Give students blank paper to lightly draw a proportional face self-portrait. (They may refer to a mirror at any time.)

3. This portrait is a representation of themselves, but only the proportions need to be accurate, colors can be representational or not.

4. Students reflect and identify the steps to create a proportional face.

Supplies needed:

Art journals, white paper 9x12 or larger, oil pastels, mirrors.

step a  step b 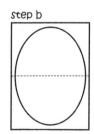 step c 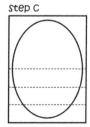 step d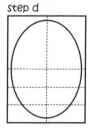

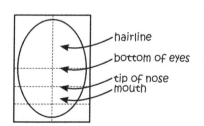
hairline
bottom of eyes
tip of nose
mouth

Objectives:

Students will learn about Pablo Picasso and his art. They will create art containing collages of color planes that represent everyday objects.

Procedures:

1. Read aloud the summary about Picasso, stopping to answer and ask questions.

2. View several works by Picasso, and discuss his planes of color.

3. Tell students to choose their favorite color and write it down. This is the main color to their art (black and white not allowed).

4. Choose several everyday objects and arrange them in a group for all to use.

5. Students sketch their picture in their art journal's first and then when ready, lightly draw it on white paper.

6. Give students colored construction and tissue papers to cut into their planes of color.

7. Students glue paper planes, and if they choose, they can add dimension with pastels.

8. Share art.

Supplies needed:

Picasso summary, samples of his work (available at www.evisualart.com), art journals, white paper 9x12 or larger, colored construction and tissue papers, scissors, glue, oil pastels.

PABLO PICASSO

(1881-1973) Spain

Pablo Picasso was educated in the styles of art of his time at an early age. His art style shifted as he experimented with different ways of visual expression. Picasso was also inspired by other artist before him and of his time.

Picasso wanted to find new ways to represent the human form, and created differing planes that broke up the solid form. He also experimented with color. Between the years of 1901-1905, he used mainly blue colors in his work. This time in Picasso's life has become known as his Blue Period.

Picasso also altered the view of the figures, representing them in more than one position at a time. His figures are not locked into one position, and have a sense of movement, time and space all at once. Picasso didn't just paint planes of color, he also used the technique of collage to represent different layers, planes and textures.

Objectives:

Students will create self-portraits that are not realistic, and based on either the style of Matisse or Picasso, or a combination of the two.

Procedures:

1. Review knowledge of Matisse and Picasso.

2. Students sketch ideas for their art piece in their art journals first. They can create their art piece in the style of Matisse or Picasso, or a combination of the two.

3. Students use pastels to depict their portrait.

4. Students write about why they chose their style and reflect on their work.

Supplies needed:

Art journals, white paper 9x12 or larger, oil pastels.

Student Name _____

Lesson	Participation	Completion	Art Journal	
LESSON 1 Wheels of Color	1 2 3 4 5 Total _____	1 2 3 4 5 (10)		_____ _____
LESSON 2 Complementary Experiment	1 2 3 4 5 Total _____	1 2 3 4 5 (15)	1 2 3 4 5	_____ _____
LESSON 3 Van Gogh's Expression	1 2 3 4 5 Total _____	1 2 3 4 5 (10)		_____ _____
LESSON 4 Non-Representational Color	1 2 3 4 5 Total _____	1 2 3 4 5 (10)		_____ _____
LESSON 5 3-Dimensional Space	1 2 3 4 5 Total _____	1 2 3 4 5 (15)	1 2 3 4 5	_____ _____
LESSON 6 Faces	1 2 3 4 5 Total _____	1 2 3 4 5 (15)	1 2 3 4 5	_____ _____
LESSON 7 Picasso Planes	1 2 3 4 5 Total _____	1 2 3 4 5 (10)		_____ _____
LESSON 8 Distortion	1 2 3 4 5 Total _____	1 2 3 4 5 (15)	1 2 3 4 5	_____

10 POINTS:
A = 9-10
B = 7-8
C = 6
D = 5

15 POINTS:
A = 13-15
B = 11-12
C = 9-10
D = 8

UNIT TOTAL (100):
A = 88-100
B = 72-87
C = 60-71
D = 56-59

Participation: student's participation during the lesson.
Completion: student's work - did they follow directions, finish the assignment, show self-expression.
Art Journal: student has written about the lesson.

The following pages are lesson plans for grade five. The lessons build off each other and include objectives, procedures and supplies needed.

Objectives:
Students will learn what one-point perspective is and use it to create the illusion of space.

Procedures:
1. Show samples of one-point perspective (picture with one vanishing point only).
2. Pass out blanks sheets of paper and rulers to students. Have them follow along on their paper with the steps of creating a simple room scene.

   Steps:
   a. Draw a rectangle that fills most of the paper.
   b. Lightly draw lines that connect the corners to a central point in the middle.
   c. Draw a smaller rectangle in the center that represents the back of the room.
   d. Now draw a door and windows and on the side walls and other objects that directly line up with the vanishing point. (There are sites online that can show you steps if needed)

3. Allow students to add other objects or practice with a new scene or color their original scene.

Supplies needed:
Art journals, white paper 9x12 or larger, ruler, pencil.

grade
5

Lesson 2 - M.C. Escher

page
100

VISUAL ART
for the elementary classroom

Objectives:

Students will learn about M.C. Escher and his work. Students will create expressive compositions using perspective and imaginary.

Procedures:

1. Read aloud the summary about Escher, stopping to answer and ask questions.

2. View several works by Escher, and discuss his impossible constructions.

3. Describe other types of perspective (two and three point) and allow students to create an image of their choice. They can create real piece or imaginary, but they need to create the illusion of space.

4. Share student art.

5. Students reflect about perspective and M.C. Escher in their art journals.

Supplies needed:

M.C. Escher summary, samples of his art (available at www.evisualart.com), art journals, white paper 9x12 or larger, rulers, pencils.

VISUAL ART
for the elementary classroom

page
101

Lesson 2 - M.C. Escher

grade
5

M.C. ESCHER

(1898-1972) Netherlands

M.C. Escher was a graphic artist who create impossible constructions. He traveled throughout Europe, but created his works through expression of his mind and not the places he had visited. Escher explored mathematical shapes and dimensions in his work, which was done in primarily black and white to enhance the dimension of his art.

M.C. Escher also created "tessellations" which are repeating of shapes or other elements, creating a pattern with the objects. He was inspired by symmetry and order, and used them in his geometric patterns.

grade
5

Lesson 3 - Quick Draw

page
102

VISUAL ART
for the elementary classroom

Objectives:

Students will describe and create gesture and contour drawings.

Procedures:

1. Explain what contour and gesture drawings are. Contour drawings are outline drawings, focusing only on the line created by the object. Blind contour drawings are done without looking at the paper and use one continuous line. Gesture drawings are quick sketches and are typically of the human figure.

2. Pass out paper, and have students draw or fold it into 8 parts.

3. Have 8 different students act as a different model for each of the 8 drawings. Students have one minute to sketch the figure the see. They need to concentrate on the motion of the figure and add no details to their drawing.

4. Post student gesture drawings for all to review, and discuss what they have learned about this form of drawing.

5. Assemble several objects for students to observe for their contour drawings. First have students divide a blank paper in two. On the first side, students use the method of blind contour to create their drawing. Give them about 5 minutes to create this drawing. On the other side, students are able to look at their paper as they draw.

6. Students compare their two drawings, and share them.

7. Students reflect in their art journals.

Supplies needed:

Art journals, white paper 9x12 or larger, objects for contour drawing, pencils or oil pastels.

Objectives:
Students will learn about René Magritte and his art. They will also create expressive abstract compositions based on real objects.

Procedures:

1. Tell students to close their eyes and have them think of several objects, which the quickly write in their art journal. Next, have them think of a place, and write that down. They will use this in step 4.

2. Read aloud the summary about Magritte, stopping to answer and ask questions.

3. View several works by Magritte, allowing students to question his art.

4. Students sketch a surreal scene based on their answers from step 1.

5. Once they have sketched their scene, they then use blank paper to create their final piece, they can use any medium they want.

6. Students reflect on Magritte and Surreal art in their art journals.

Supplies needed:
Summary of Magritte, samples of his art (available at www.evisualart.com), art journals, white paper 9x12 or larger, tempera paints, paint brushes, oil pastels and watercolors.

grade
5

Lesson 4 - Surreal Art

page
104

VISUAL ART
for the elementary classroom

RENÉ MAGRITTE

(1898-1967) Belgium

René Magritte studied art at an early age, even attending the Brussels Academy of Fine Arts. He was influenced by other abstract movements of the past and during his time. Magritte developed a style of art that is known as Surrealism. Surreal artists try to show altered conceptions of reality and challenge the viewer's preconceived knowledge of their surroundings.

Magritte would take ordinary objects and create new realities with them. He would experiment with objects and scenes, developing scenes that make the viewer uncomfortable. Although he experimented with common reality, Magritte painted his scenes and objects as they actually look.

VISUAL ART
for the elementary classroom
page
105
Lesson 5 - Monet
grade
5

Objectives:

Students will learn about Claude Monet and his art and will compare his work to realities of the environment. Students will also create a landscape that is in the impressionist style.

Procedures:

1. Read aloud the summary about Monet, stopping to answer and ask questions.

2. View several works by Monet, noting the differences in colors and paint strokes of color.

3. Tell students that they are going to create Money style landscape. Show them how to paint with pieces of sponges, creating an imperfect stroke.

4. Pass out white paper and students will draw their landscape first before painting.

5. Students share their art and reflect in their art journals.

Supplies needed:

Summary of Monet, samples of his art (available at www.evisualart.com), art journals, white paper 9x12 or larger, tempera paints, sponges cut to about 2 x 1/2 inches.

CLAUDE MONET

(1840-1926) France

Claude Monet was interested in becoming an artist, but his parents refused to support him and his plans. Early in his career, he had to support himself by begging for help from his friends. Finally at the age of 50, Monet was financially successful.

Monet was obsessed with color and light. He chose to work outdoors, and would paint scenes over and over from the same point of view at different times of day and different seasons. Monet understood that color changes from the morning to night, from winter to summer, cloudy day to sunny day, and he worked to represent the passage of time.

Monet painted with small strokes of color, allowing the viewer's eye to blend the colors together. He did not just use pure color, and included tints and shades of color into his work to help depict the time or mood of his art.

VISUAL ART
for the elementary classroom

page
107

Lesson 6 - Mixed Media

grade
5

Objectives:

Students will create a mixed media art piece that communicates a theme.

Procedures:

1. Discuss what mixed media is and how artists use it to communicate expression.

2. Show students varying types of paper that they can use to assemble their piece. They can also use tempera paints and oil pastels.

3. Students decide on a theme, and sketch their initial ideas in their art journals. Once finished, they lightly draw on white paper, and gather the materials that they want to use.

4. Share student art and have students reflect on the process of creating mixed media art and how it differs from using just one medium.

Supplies needed:

Art journals, white paper 9x12 or larger, tempera paints, paint brushes, colored construction and tissue papers, scissors, glue, oil pastels.

grade
5

Lesson 7 - Icons and Logos

page
108

VISUAL ART
for the elementary classroom

Objectives:

Students will identify and design an icon or logo.

Procedures:

1. Show students logos that are on everyday objects.

2. Discuss what makes a good logo, based on the ones they have just viewed. Write these attributes.

3. Group students in to groups of 4-5. Tell them they are creating a company that determines what is good art. In their group they need to agree on a name and then form a logo or icon for their company. They choose colors as well.

4. Students share their company name and logo with the class. They will use this for the next lesson.

Supplies needed:

Art journals, white paper, tempera paints, paint brushes, oil pastels, markers.

VISUAL ART
for the elementary classroom

page
109

Lesson 8 - What is Good Art?

grade
5

Objectives:

Students will work to identify, describe and define what they believe makes good art. They will use their knowledge about artists, art elements and art creation to determine criteria for assessing works of art.

Procedures:

1. Students form their groups from lesson 7.

2. Lead a discussion on what makes a good piece of art. These are their beliefs, and should be also based on their prior learned art knowledge.

3. Students work together to create guidelines for assessing art.

4. Students present their companies guidelines and show a piece they have determined to be good, and one determined to not meet their criteria.

Supplies needed:

Art journals, works of art samples, lined paper.

Student Name _____

Lesson	Participation	Completion	Art Journal	
LESSON 1 One-Point Perspective	1 2 3 4 5 Total _____	1 2 3 4 5 (15)	1 2 3 4 5	_____ _____
LESSON 2 M.C. Escher	1 2 3 4 5 Total _____	1 2 3 4 5 (15)	1 2 3 4 5	_____ _____
LESSON 3 Quick Draw	1 2 3 4 5 Total _____	1 2 3 4 5 (15)	1 2 3 4 5	_____ _____
LESSON 4 Surreal Art	1 2 3 4 5 Total _____	1 2 3 4 5 (15)	1 2 3 4 5	_____ _____
LESSON 5 Monet	1 2 3 4 5 Total _____	1 2 3 4 5 (15)	1 2 3 4 5	_____ _____
LESSON 6 Mixed Media	1 2 3 4 5 Total _____	1 2 3 4 5 (15)	1 2 3 4 5	_____ _____
LESSON 7 Icons and Logos	1 2 3 4 5 Total _____	1 2 3 4 5 (15)	Group work: 1 2 3 4 5	_____
LESSON 8 What is Good Art?	Group participation: Guidelines for assessing art: Group presentation: Total _____ (30)		1 2 3 4 5 6 7 8 9 10 1 2 3 4 5 6 7 8 9 10 1 2 3 4 5 6 7 8 9 10	_____

15 POINTS:	30 POINTS:	UNIT TOTAL (135):
A = 14-15	A = 27-30	A = 125-135
B = 12-13	B = 24-26	B = 108-124
C = 10-11	C = 21-23	C = 91-107
D = 8-9	D = 18-20	D = 74-90

Participation: student's participation during the lesson.
Completion: student's work - did they follow directions, finish the assignment, show self-expression.
Art Journal: student has written about the lesson.

VISUAL ART
for the elementary classroom
page
111
Art Terms and References
grades
K-5

Primary colors: colors that can not be made by mixing other colors; red, yellow and blue.

Secondary colors: colors made be mixing 2 primary colors; orange, green and violet.

Complementary colors: colors that are opposites on the color wheel and create neutrals when mixed together.

Tertiary colors: colors made by mixing a primary color with a secondary color; red–orange, orange-yellow, yellow-green, green-blue, blue-violet, violet-red.

Neutral colors: shades and tints of black and white, creating greys.

Tint: color mixed with white.

Tone: color mixed with gray.

Shade: color mixed with black.

Hue: pure color, except black and white, with no tint or shade.

Value: the lightness of a color, with high value colors being close to white and low value colors being close to black.

Warm colors: reds through yellows, including brown and tan.

Cool colors: blue-green through violet, including greys.

One-point perspective: a scene with only one vanishing point.

Two-point perspective: a scene with two vanishing points.

Bilateral symmetry: on one plane, a mirror image on both sides.

Radial symmetry: on multiple planes, mirroring images.

REFERENCES

De la Croix, H., Tansey, R., Kirkpatrick, D. (1991). Gardner's art through the ages, ninth edition. Fort Worth, TX: Harcourt Brace Jovanovich College Publishers.

Canaday, J. (1981). Mainstreams in modern art, second edition. Fort Worth, TX: Harcourt Brace Jovanovich College Publishers.

California Standards from: http://www.cde.ca.gov/be/st/ss/vamain.asp

Nevada Standards from: http://www.doe.nv.gov/Standards_Arts_Visual.html

grades
K-1

California Standards

page
112

visual art
for the elementary classroom

KINDERGARTEN

Lesson 1 - Color Basics

1.2 - Name art materials (e.g., clay, paint, and crayons) introduced in lessons.

1.3 - Identify the elements of art (line, color, shape/form, texture, value, space) in the environment and in works of art, emphasizing line, color, and shape/form.

2.2 - Demonstrate beginning skill in the use of tools and processes, such as the use of scissors, glue, and paper in creating a three-dimensional construction.

Lesson 2 - Shapes

1.3 - Identify the elements of art (line, color, shape/form, texture, value, space) in the environment and in works of art, emphasizing line, color, and shape/form.

2.6 - Use geometric shapes/forms (circle, triangle, square) in a work of art.

Lesson 3 - Textures

1.1 - Recognize and describe simple patterns found in the environment and works of art.

1.3 - Identify the elements of art (line, color, shape/form, texture, value, space) in the environment and in works of art, emphasizing line, color, and shape/form.

2.1 - Use lines, shapes/forms, and colors to make patterns.

Lesson 4 - Dancing Shapes

1.1 - Recognize and describe simple patterns found in the environment and works of art.

2.1 - Use lines, shapes/forms, and colors to make patterns.

5.1 - Draw geometric shapes/forms (e.g., circles, squares, triangles) and repeat them in dance/movement sequences.

Lesson 5 - Bugs 2D

1.3 - Identify the elements of art (line, color, shape/form, texture, value, space) in the environment and in works of art, emphasizing line, color, and shape/form.

2.2 - Demonstrate beginning skill in the use of tools and processes, such as the use of scissors, glue, and paper in creating a three-dimensional construction.

2.3 - Make a collage with cut or torn paper shapes/forms.

2.6 - Use geometric shapes/forms (circle, triangle, square) in a work of art.

4.1 - Discuss their own works of art, using appropriate art vocabulary (e.g., color, shape/form, texture).

Lesson 6 - Bugs 3D

1.2 - Name art materials (e.g., clay, paint, and crayons) introduced in lessons.

1.3 - Identify the elements of art (line, color, shape/form, texture, value, space) in the environment and in works of art, emphasizing line, color, and shape/form.

2.2 - Demonstrate beginning skill in the use of tools and processes, such as the use of scissors, glue, and paper in creating a three-dimensional construction.

2.6 - Use geometric shapes/forms (circle, triangle, square) in a work of art.

2.7 - Create a three-dimensional form, such as a real or imaginary animal.

4.4 - Give reasons why they like a particular work of art they made, using appropriate art vocabulary.

Lesson 7 - Everyday Objects

1.2 - Name art materials (e.g., clay, paint, and crayons) introduced in lessons.

1.3 - Identify the elements of art (line, color, shape/form, texture, value, space) in the environment and in works of art, emphasizing line, color, and shape/form.

2.1 - Use lines, shapes/forms, and colors to make patterns.

4.3 - Discuss how and why they made a specific work of art.

5.2 - Look at and draw something used every day (e.g., scissors, toothbrush, fork) and describe how the object is used.

Lesson 8 - Our Town: Places

1.2 - Name art materials (e.g., clay, paint, and crayons) introduced in lessons.

1.3 - Identify the elements of art (line, color, shape/form, texture, value, space) in the environment and in works of art, emphasizing line, color, and shape/form.

2.2 - Demonstrate beginning skill in the use of tools and processes, such as the use of scissors, glue, and paper in creating a three-dimensional construction.

Lesson 9 - Our Town: People

1.1 - Recognize and describe simple patterns found in the environment and works of art.

1.2 - Name art materials (e.g., clay, paint, and crayons) introduced in lessons.

1.3 - Identify the elements of art (line, color, shape/form, texture, value, space) in the environment and in works of art, emphasizing line, color, and shape/form.

2.1 - Use lines, shapes/forms, and colors to make patterns.

2.2 - Demonstrate beginning skill in the use of tools and processes, such as the use of scissors, glue, and paper in creating a three-dimensional construction.

2.3 - Make a collage with cut or torn paper shapes/forms.

2.4 - Paint pictures expressing ideas about family and neighborhood.

2.5 - Use lines in drawings and paintings to express feelings.

GRADE 1

Lesson 1 - Secondary Colors

2.2 - Mix secondary colors from primary colors and describe the process.

Lesson 2 - Secondary Still Life

2.2 - Mix secondary colors from primary colors and describe the process.

2.6 - Draw or paint a still life, using secondary colors.

2.8 - Create artwork based on observations of actual objects and everyday scenes.

3.2 - Identify and describe various subject matter in art (e.g., landscapes, seascapes, portraits, still life).

4.4 - Select something they like about their work of art and something they would change.

Lesson 3 - Still Life 3D

1.2 - Distinguish among various media when looking at works of art (e.g., clay, paints, drawing materials).

2.1 - Use texture in two-dimensional and three-dimensional works of art.

2.3 - Demonstrate beginning skill in the manipulation and use of sculptural materials (clay, paper and paper maché) to create form and texture in works of art.

2.5 - Create a representational sculpture based on people animals, or buildings.

2.7 - Use visual and actual texture in original works of art.

2.8 - Create artwork based on observations of actual objects and everyday scenes.

3.2 - Identify and describe various subject matter in art (e.g., landscapes, seascapes, portraits, still life).

4.3 - Describe how and why they made a selected work of art, focusing on the media and technique.

Lesson 4 - Vasarely Repetition

1.1 - Describe and replicate repeated patterns in nature, in the environment, and in works of art.

1.2 - Distinguish among various media when looking at works of art (e.g., clay, paints, drawing materials).

2.1 - Use texture in two-dimensional and three-dimensional works of art.

2.4 - Plan and use variations in line, shape/form, color, and texture to communicate ideas or feelings in works of art.

2.7 - Use visual and actual texture in original works of art.

4.1 - Discuss works of art created in the classroom, focusing on selected elements of art (e.g., shape/form, texture, line, color).

Lesson 5 - Rhythmic Patterns

1.1 - Describe and replicate repeated patterns in nature, in the environment, and in works of art.

5.1 - Clap out rhythmic patterns found in the lyrics of music and use symbols to create visual representations of the patterns.

Lesson 6 - Patterns in Nature

1.1 - Describe and replicate repeated patterns in nature, in the environment, and in works of art.

1.3 - Identify the elements of art in objects in nature, the environment, and works of art, emphasizing line, color, shape/form, and texture.

2.1 - Use texture in two-dimensional and three-dimensional works of art.

2.3 - Demonstrate beginning skill in the manipulation and use of sculptural materials (clay, paper and paper maché) to create form and texture in works of art.

2.4 - Plan and use variations in line, shape/form, color, and texture to communicate ideas or feelings in works of art.

2.7 - Use visual and actual texture in original works of art.

2.8 - Create artwork based on observations of actual objects and everyday scenes.

Lesson 7 - Why We Create Art

1.1 - Describe and replicate repeated patterns in nature, in the environment, and in works of art.

1.3 - Identify the elements of art in objects in nature, the environment, and works of art, emphasizing line, color, shape/form, and texture.

2.1 - Use texture in two-dimensional and three-dimensional works of art.

2.4 - Plan and use variations in line, shape/form, color, and texture to communicate ideas or feelings in works of art.

2.7 - Use visual and actual texture in original works of art.

4.2 - Identify and describe various reasons for making art.

5.3 - Identify and sort pictures into categories according to the elements of art emphasized in the works (e.g., color, line, shape/form, texture).

Lesson 8 - Why I Create Art

1.1 - Describe and replicate repeated patterns in nature, in the environment, and in works of art.

1.3 - Identify the elements of art in objects in nature, the environment, and works of art, emphasizing line, color, shape/form, and texture.

2.1 - Use texture in two-dimensional and three-dimensional works of art.

2.4 - Plan and use variations in line, shape/form, color, and texture to communicate ideas or feelings in works of art.

2.7 - Use visual and actual texture in original works of art.

2.8 - Create artwork based on observations of actual objects and everyday scenes.

4.3 - Describe how and why they made a selected work of art, focusing on the media and techniques.

4.4 - Select something like about their work of art and something they would change.

GRADE 2

Lesson 1 - Warm Colors

1.2 - Perceive and discuss differences in mood created by warm and cool colors.

1.3 - Identify the elements of art in objects in nature, the environment, and works of art, emphasizing line, color, shape/form, texture and shape.

2.1 - Demonstrate beginning skill in the use of basic tools and art-making processes, such as printing, crayon rubbings, collage, and stencils.

2.4 - Create a painting or drawing, using warm or cool colors expressively.

Lesson 2 - Cool Colors

1.2 - Perceive and discuss differences in mood created by warm and cool colors.

1.3 - Identify the elements of art in objects in nature, the environment, and works of art, emphasizing line, color, shape/form, texture and shape.

2.2 - Demonstrate beginning skill in the use of art media, such as oil pastels, watercolors, and tempera.

2.4 - Create a painting or drawing, using warm or cool colors expressively.

Lesson 3 - Warm vs. Cool

1.2 - Perceive and discuss differences in mood created by warm and cool colors.

2.2 - Demonstrate beginning skill in the use of art media, such as oil pastels, watercolors, and tempera.

2.4 - Create a painting or drawing, using warm or cool colors expressively.

4.1 - Compare ideas expressed through their own works of art with ideas expressed in the work of others.

4.2 - Compare different responses to the same work of art.

5.3 - Identify pictures and sort them into categories according to expressive qualities (e.g., theme and mood).

Lesson 4 - Found in Nature

1.1 - Perceive and describe repetition and balance in nature, in the environment, and in works of art.

1.3 - Identify the elements of art in objects in nature, the environment, and works of art, emphasizing line, color, shape/form, texture and shape.

2.1 - Demonstrate beginning skill in the use of basic tools and art-making processes, such as printing, crayon rubbings, collage, and stencils.

Lesson 5 - Jasper Johns

1.1 - Perceive and describe repetition and balance in nature, in the environment, and in works of art.

1.3 - Identify the elements of art in objects in nature, the environment, and works of art, emphasizing line, color, shape/form, texture and shape.

2.1 - Demonstrate beginning skill in the use of basic tools and art-making processes, such as printing, crayon rubbings, collage, and stencils.

2.2 - Demonstrate beginning skill in the use of art media, such as oil pastels, watercolors, and tempera.

2.3 - Depict the illusion of depth (space) in a work of art, using overlapping shapes, relative size, and placement within the picture.

5.1 - Use placement, overlapping, and size differences to show opposites (e.g., up/down, in/out, over/under, together/apart, fast/slow, stop/go).

Lesson 6 - Repetition with Nature

1.1 - Perceive and describe repetition and balance in nature, in the environment, and in works of art.

1.3 - Identify the elements of art in objects in nature, the environment, and works of art, emphasizing line, color, shape/form, texture and shape.

2.1 - Demonstrate beginning skill in the use of basic tools and art-making processes, such as printing, crayon rubbings, collage, and stencils.

2.2 - Demonstrate beginning skill in the use of art media, such as oil pastels, watercolors, and tempera.

2.3 - Depict the illusion of depth (space) in a work of art, using overlapping shapes, relative size, and placement within the picture.

5.1 - Use placement, overlapping, and size differences to show opposites (e.g., up/down, in/out, over/under, together/apart, fast/slow, stop/go).

Lesson 7 - Andy Warhol

2.2 - Demonstrate beginning skill in the use of art media, such as oil pastels, watercolors, and tempera.

3.2 - Recognize and use the vocabulary of art to describe art objects from various cultures and time periods.

5.2 - Select and use expressive colors to create mood and show personality within a portrait of a hero from long ago or the recent past.

Lesson 8 - Warhol Warm and Cool

1.2 - Perceive and discuss differences in mood created by warm and cool colors.

2.2 - Demonstrate beginning skill in the use of art media, such as oil pastels, watercolors, and tempera.

2.4 - Create a painting or drawing, using warm and cool colors expressively.

4.3 - Use the vocabulary of art to talk about what they wanted to do in their own works of art and how they succeeded.

4.4 - Use appropriate vocabulary of art to describe the successful use of an element of art in a work of art.

5.2 - Select and use expressive colors to create mood and show personality within a portrait of a hero from long ago or the recent past.

5.3 - Identify pictures and sort them into categories according to expressive qualities (e.g., theme and mood).

Lesson 9 - Camouflage?

2.2 - Demonstrate beginning skill in the use of art media, such as oil pastels, watercolors, and tempera.

3.1 - Explain how artists use their work to share experiences or communicate ideas.

3.2 - Recognize and use the vocabulary of art to describe art objects from various cultures and time periods.

4.1 - Compare ideas expressed through their own works of art with ideas expressed in the work of art.

4.2 - Compare different responses to the same work of art.

Lesson 10 - What I Know

3.1 - Explain how artists use their work to share experiences or communicate ideas.

3.2 - Recognize and use the vocabulary of art to describe art objects from various cultures and time periods.

3.3 - Identify and discuss how art is used in events and celebrations in various cultures, past and present, including the use in their own lives.

4.1 - Compare ideas expressed through their own works of art with ideas expressed in the work of art.

GRADE 3

Lesson 1 - Primary Mondrian

1.5 - Identify and describe elements of art in works of art, emphasizing line, color, shape/form, texture, space, and value.

2.1 - Explore ideas for art in a personal sketchbook.

3.3 - Distinguish and describe representational, abstract, and nonrepresentational works of art.

Lesson 2 - Tints, Shades and Neutrals

1.5 - Identify and describe elements of art in works of art, emphasizing line, color, shape/form, texture, space, and value.

2.1 - Explore ideas for art in a personal sketchbook.

2.2 - Mix and apply tempera paints to create tints, shades, and neutral colors.

Lesson 3 - Seurat Dots

1.1 - Perceive and describe rhythm and movement in works of art and in the environment.

1.2 - Describe how artists use tints and shades in painting.

1.3 - Identify and describe how foreground, middle ground, and background are used to create the illusion of space.

1.5 - Identify and describe elements of art in works of art, emphasizing line, color, shape/form, texture, space, and value.

2.1 - Explore ideas for art in a personal sketchbook.

Lesson 4 - Mondrian vs. Seurat

1.1 - Perceive and describe rhythm and movement in works of art and in the environment.

1.4 - Compare and contrast two works of art made by the use of different art tools and media (e.g., watercolor, tempera, computer).

1.5 - Identify and describe elements of art in works of art, emphasizing line, color, shape/form, texture, space, and value.

3.1 - Compare and describe various works of art that have a similar theme and were created at different time periods.

4.1 - Compare and contrast selected works of art and describe them, using appropriate vocabulary of art.

Lesson 5 - Illusions of Space Scapes

1.3 - Identify and describe how foreground, middle ground, and background are used to create the illusion of space.

2.1 - Explore ideas for art in a personal sketchbook.

2.2 - Mix and apply tempera paints to create tints, shades, and neutral colors.

2.3 - Paint or draw a landscape, seascape, or cityscape that shows the illusion of space.

2.6 - Create an original work of art emphasizing rhythm and movement, using a selected printing process.

5.2 - Write a poem or story inspired by their own works of art.

Lesson 6 - Warm and Cool

1.3 - Identify and describe how foreground, middle ground, and background are used to create the illusion of space.

2.1 - Explore ideas for art in a personal sketchbook.

Lesson 7 - Cezanne

1.1 - Perceive and describe rhythm and movement in works of art and in the environment.

1.3 - Identify and describe how foreground, middle ground, and background are used to create the illusion of space.

2.1 - Explore ideas for art in a personal sketchbook.

2.3 - Paint or draw a landscape, seascape, or cityscape that shows the illusion of space.

2.4 - Create a work of art based on the observation of objects and scenes in daily life, emphasizing value changes.

2.6 - Create an original work of art emphasizing rhythm and movement, using a selected printing process.

Lesson 8 - What Happens Next?

2.1 - Explore ideas for art in a personal sketchbook.

2.6 - Create an original work of art emphasizing rhythm and movement, using a selected printing process.

5.3 - Look at images in figurative works of art and predict what might happen next, telling what clues in the work support their ideas.

Lesson 9 - Why is Art Important?

1.2 - Describe how artists use tints and shades in painting.

1.3 - Identify and describe how foreground, middle ground, and background are used to create the illusion of space.

1.5 - Identify and describe elements of art in works of art, emphasizing line, color, shape/form, texture, space, and value.

4.3 - Select an artist's work and, using appropriate vocabulary of art, explain its successful compositional and communicative qualities.

Lesson 10 - What I Know

2.1 - Explore ideas for art in a personal sketchbook.

2.2 - Mix and apply tempera paints to create tints, shades, and neutral colors.

2.6 - Create an original work of art emphasizing rhythm and movement, using a selected printing process.

GRADE 4

Lesson 1 - Wheels of Color

1.3 - Identify pairs of complementary colors (yellow/violet; red/green; orange/blue) and discuss how artists use them to communicate an idea or mood.

Lesson 2 - Complementary Experiment

1.3 - Identify pairs of complementary colors (yellow/violet; red/green; orange/blue) and discuss how artists use them to communicate an idea or mood.

Lesson 3 - Van Gogh's Expression

1.3 - Identify pairs of complementary colors (yellow/violet; red/green; orange/blue) and discuss how artists use them to communicate an idea or mood.

1.5 - Describe and analyze the elements of art (color, shape/form, line, texture, space, value), emphasizing form, as they are used in works of art and found in the environment.

2.7 - Use contrast (light and dark) expressively in an original work of art.

2.8 - Use complementary colors in an original composition to show contrast and emphasis.

Lesson 4 - Non-Representational Color

1.2 - Describe how negative shapes/forms and positive shapes/forms are used in a chosen work of art.

2.6 - Use the interaction between positive and negative space expressively in a work of art.

2.7 - Use contrast (light and dark) expressively in an original work of art.

Lesson 5 - 3-Dimensional Space

1.2 - Describe how negative shapes/forms and positive shapes/forms are used in a chosen work of art.

2.1 - Use shading (value) to transform a two-dimensional shape into what appears to be a three-dimensional form (e.g., circle to sphere).

2.6 - Use the interaction between positive and negative space expressively in a work of art.

2.7 - Use contrast (light and dark) expressively in an original work of art.

Lesson 6 - Faces

2.2 - Use the conventions of facial and figure proportions in a figure study.

2.5 - Use accurate proportions to create an expressive portrait or a figure drawing or painting.

Lesson 7 - Picasso Planes

2.1 - Use shading (value) to transform a two-dimensional shape into what appears to be a three-dimensional form (e.g., circle to sphere).

2.7 - Use contrast (light and dark) expressively in an original work of art.

Lesson 8 - Distortions

1.5 - Describe and analyze the elements of art (color, shape/form, line, texture, space, value), emphasizing form, as they are used in works of art and found in the environment.

2.7 - Use contrast (light and dark) expressively in an original work of art.

GRADE 5

Lesson 1 - One-Point Perspective

2.1 - Use one-point perspective to create the illusion of space.

2.6 - Use perspective in an original work of art to create a real or imaginary scene.

5.1 - Use linear perspective to depict geometric objects in space.

Lesson 2 - M.C. Escher

2.4 - Create an expressive abstract composition based on real objects.

2.6 - Use perspective in an original work of art to create a real or imaginary scene.

5.1 - Use linear perspective to depict geometric objects in space.

Lesson 3 - Quick Draw

2.2 - Create gesture and contour observational drawings.

Lesson 4 - Surreal Art

2.4 - Create an expressive abstract composition based on real objects.

2.7 - Communicate values, opinions, or personal insights through an original work of art.

Lesson 5 - Monet

1.1 - Identify and describe the principles of design in visual compositions, emphasizing unity and harmony.

1.2 - Identify and describe characteristics of representational, abstract, and nonrepresentational works of art.

1.3 - Use their knowledge of all the elements of art to describe similarities and differences in works of art and in the environment.

Lesson 6 - Mixed Media

2.5 - Assemble a found object sculpture (as assemblage) or a mixed media two-dimensional composition that reflects unity and harmony and communicates a theme.

Lesson 7 - Icons and Logos

5.2 - Identify and design icons, logos, and other graphic devices as symbols for ideas and information.

Lesson 8 - What is Good Art?

1.1 - Identify and describe the principles of design in visual compositions, emphasizing unity and harmony.

1.3 - Use their knowledge of all the elements of art to describe similarities and differences in works of art and in the environment.

4.1 - Identify how selected principles of design are used in a work of art and how they affect personal responses to and evaluation of the work of art.

4.3 - Develop and use specific criteria as individuals and in groups to assess works of art.

4.4 - Assess their own works of art, using specific criteria, and describe what changes they would make for improvement.

GRADE 1

Lesson 1 - Secondary Colors

2.3.1 - Identify selected elements of design and principles of design in nature and in works of art.

Lesson 2 - Secondary Still Life

1.3.3 - Use different media, techniques, and processes to produce works of art.

2.3.1 - Identify selected elements of design and principles of design in nature and in works of art.

2.3.4 - Use elements and principals of design to create works of art.

Lesson 3 - Still Life 3D

1.3.3 - Use different media, techniques, and processes to produce works of art.

2.3.1 - Identify selected elements of design and principles of design in nature and in works of art.

2.3.4 - Use elements and principals of design to create works of art.

Lesson 4 - Vasarely Repetition

1.3.3 - Use different media, techniques, and processes to produce works of art.

2.3.1 - Identify selected elements of design and principles of design in nature and in works of art.

2.3.4 - Use elements and principals of design to create works of art.

Lesson 5 - Rhythmic Patterns

2.3.1 - Identify selected elements of design and principles of design in nature and in works of art.

Lesson 6 - Patterns in Nature

1.3.3 - Use different media, techniques, and processes to produce works of art.

2.3.1 - Identify selected elements of design and principles of design in nature and in works of art.

2.3.4 - Use elements and principals of design to create works of art.

Lesson 7 - Why We Create Art

1.3.3 - Use different media, techniques, and processes to produce works of art.

2.3.1 - Identify selected elements of design and principles of design in nature and in works of art.

2.3.4 - Use elements and principals of design to create works of art.

Lesson 8 - Why I Create Art

1.3.3 - Use different media, techniques, and processes to produce works of art.

2.3.1 - Identify selected elements of design and principles of design in nature and in works of art.

2.3.4 - Use elements and principals of design to create works of art.

GRADE 2

Lesson 1 - Warm Colors

1.3.3 - Use different media, techniques, and processes to produce works of art.

2.3.4 - Use elements and principle of design to create works of art.

Lesson 2 - Cool Colors

1.3.3 - Use different media, techniques, and processes to produce works of art.

2.3.4 - Use elements and principle of design to create works of art.

Lesson 3 - Warm vs. Cool

1.3.3 - Use different media, techniques, and processes to produce works of art.

2.3.4 - Use elements and principle of design to create works of art.

Lesson 4 - Found in Nature

1.3.3 - Use different media, techniques, and processes to produce works of art.

2.3.4 - Use elements and principle of design to create works of art.

Lesson 5 - Jasper Johns

1.3.3 - Use different media, techniques, and processes to produce works of art.

2.3.1 - Identify selected elements of design and principles of design in nature and in works of art.

2.3.4 - Use elements and principle of design to create works of art.

Lesson 6 - Repetition with Nature

1.3.3 - Use different media, techniques, and processes to produce works of art.

2.3.1 - Identify selected elements of design and principals of design in nature and in works of art.

2.3.4 - Use elements and principle of design to create works of art.

3.3.2 - Create artwork that demonstrates choice of subject matter and symbols to communicate meaning.

Lesson 7 - Andy Warhol

1.3.3 - Use different media, techniques, and processes to produce works of art.

2.3.1 - Identify selected elements of design and principals of design in nature and in works of art.

2.3.4 - Use elements and principle of design to create works of art.

3.3.2 - Create artwork that demonstrates choice of subject matter and symbols to communicate meaning.

Lesson 8 - Warhol Warm and Cool

1.3.3 - Use different media, techniques, and processes to produce works of art.

2.3.1 - Identify selected elements of design and principals of design in nature and in works of art.

2.3.4 - Use elements and principle of design to create works of art.

3.3.2 - Create artwork that demonstrates choice of subject matter and symbols to communicate meaning.

Lesson 9 - Camouflage?

1.3.3 - Use different media, techniques, and processes to produce works of art.

2.3.4 - Use elements and principle of design to create works of art.

3.3.2 - Create artwork that demonstrates choice of subject matter and symbols to communicate meaning.

Lesson 10 - What I Know

1.3.3 - Use different media, techniques, and processes to produce works of art.

2.3.1 - Identify selected elements of design and principals of design in nature and in works of art.

2.3.4 - Use elements and principle of design to create works of art.

3.3.2 - Create artwork that demonstrates choice of subject matter and symbols to communicate meaning.

GRADE 3

Lesson 1 - Primary Mondrian

1.3.3 - Use different media, techniques, and processes to produce works of art.

2.3.4 - Use elements and principle of design to create works of art.

Lesson 2 - Tints, Shades and Neutrals

1.3.3 - Use different media, techniques, and processes to produce works of art.

2.3.1 - Identify selected elements of design and principals of design in nature and in works of art.

2.3.4 - Use elements and principle of design to create works of art.

Lesson 3 - Seurat Dots

1.3.3 - Use different media, techniques, and processes to produce works of art.

2.3.1 - Identify selected elements of design and principals of design in nature and in works of art.

2.3.4 - Use elements and principle of design to create works of art.

Lesson 4 - Mondrian vs. Seurat

1.3.3 - Use different media, techniques, and processes to produce works of art.

2.3.1 - Identify selected elements of design and principals of design in nature and in works of art.

2.3.4 - Use elements and principle of design to create works of art.

Lesson 5 - Illusions of Space Scapes

1.3.3 - Use different media, techniques, and processes to produce works of art.

2.3.1 - Identify selected elements of design and principals of design in nature and in works of art.

2.3.4 - Use elements and principle of design to create works of art.

3.3.2 - Create artwork that demonstrates choice of subject matter and symbols to communicate meaning.

Lesson 6 - Warm and Cool

1.3.3 - Use different media, techniques, and processes to produce works of art.

2.3.1 - Identify selected elements of design and principals of design in nature and in works of art.

2.3.4 - Use elements and principle of design to create works of art.

3.3.2 - Create artwork that demonstrates choice of subject matter and symbols to communicate meaning.

Lesson 7 - Cezanne

1.3.3 - Use different media, techniques, and processes to produce works of art.

2.3.1 - Identify selected elements of design and principals of design in nature and in works of art.

2.3.4 - Use elements and principle of design to create works of art.

3.3.2 - Create artwork that demonstrates choice of subject matter and symbols to communicate meaning.

Lesson 8 - What Happens Next?

1.3.3 - Use different media, techniques, and processes to produce works of art.

2.3.1 - Identify selected elements of design and principals of design in nature and in works of art.

2.3.4 - Use elements and principle of design to create works of art.

3.3.2 - Create artwork that demonstrates choice of subject matter and symbols to communicate meaning.

Lesson 9 - Why is Art Important?

1.3.3 - Use different media, techniques, and processes to produce works of art.

2.3.1 - Identify selected elements of design and principals of design in nature and in works of art.

2.3.4 - Use elements and principle of design to create works of art.

3.3.2 - Create artwork that demonstrates choice of subject matter and symbols to communicate meaning.

Lesson 10 - What I Know

1.3.3 - Use different media, techniques, and processes to produce works of art.

2.3.1 - Identify selected elements of design and principals of design in nature and in works of art.

2.3.4 - Use elements and principle of design to create works of art.

3.3.2 - Create artwork that demonstrates choice of subject matter and symbols to communicate meaning.

GRADE 4

Lesson 1 - Wheels of Color

1.5.3 - Create artworks using various media, techniques, and processes to communicate ideas.

Lesson 2 - Complementary Experiment

1.5.3 - Create artworks using various media, techniques, and processes to communicate ideas.

Lesson 3 - Van Gogh's Expression

1.5.3 - Create artworks using various media, techniques, and processes to communicate ideas.

2.5.1 - Describe various visual characteristics of art (e.g. sensory, formal, technical and expressive).

2.5.4 - Select and use specific visual characteristics to communicate.

Lesson 4 - Non-Representational Color

1.5.2 - Examine how different media, techniques, and processes cause different responses.

1.5.3 - Create artworks using various media, techniques, and processes to communicate ideas.

Lesson 5 - 3-Dimensional Space

1.5.3 - Create artworks using various media, techniques, and processes to communicate ideas.

2.5.1 - Describe various visual characteristics of art (e.g. sensory, formal, technical and expressive).

2.5.4 - Select and use specific visual characteristics to communicate.

5.5.1 - Compare and contrast characteristics of art.

5.5.4 - State preferences for characteristics, merits, and meanings in art.

Lesson 6 - Faces

1.5.3 - Create artworks using various media, techniques, and processes to communicate ideas.

2.5.1 - Describe various visual characteristics of art (e.g. sensory, formal, technical and expressive).

2.5.4 - Select and use specific visual characteristics to communicate.

Lesson 7 - Picasso Planes

1.5.3 - Create artworks using various media, techniques, and processes to communicate ideas.

2.5.1 - Describe various visual characteristics of art (e.g. sensory, formal, technical and expressive).

2.5.4 - Select and use specific visual characteristics to communicate.

Lesson 8 - Distortions

1.5.3 - Create artworks using various media, techniques, and processes to communicate ideas.

2.5.1 - Describe various visual characteristics of art (e.g. sensory, formal, technical and expressive).

2.5.3 - Explain how visual characteristics, purposes, and/or functions of art may cause different responses.

2.5.4 - Select and use specific visual characteristics to communicate.

GRADE 5

Lesson 1 - One-Point Perspective

1.5.3 - Create artworks using various media, techniques, and processes to communicate ideas.

2.5.1 - Describe various visual characteristics of art (e.g. sensory, formal, technical and expressive).

2.5.4 - Select and use specific visual characteristics to communicate.

Lesson 2 - M.C. Escher

1.5.3 - Create artworks using various media, techniques, and processes to communicate ideas.

2.5.1 - Describe various visual characteristics of art (e.g. sensory, formal, technical and expressive).

2.5.4 - Select and use specific visual characteristics to communicate.

Lesson 3 - Quick Draw

1.5.1 - Determine differences between media, techniques or processes in works of art.

1.5.3 - Create artworks using various media, techniques, and processes to communicate ideas.

2.5.1 - Describe various visual characteristics of art (e.g. sensory, formal, technical and expressive).

2.5.4 - Select and use specific visual characteristics to communicate.

Lesson 4 - Surreal Art

1.5.3 - Create artworks using various media, techniques, and processes to communicate ideas.

2.5.1 - Describe various visual characteristics of art (e.g. sensory, formal, technical and expressive).

2.5.3 - Explain how visual characteristics, purposes, and/or functions of art may cause different responses.

2.5.4 - Select and use specific visual characteristics to communicate.

Lesson 5 - Monet

1.5.1 - Determine differences between media, techniques or processes in works of art.

1.5.3 - Create artworks using various media, techniques, and processes to communicate ideas.

2.5.1 - Describe various visual characteristics of art (e.g. sensory, formal, technical and expressive).

2.5.4 - Select and use specific visual characteristics to communicate.

Lesson 6 - Mixed Media

1.5.1 - Determine differences between media, techniques or processes in works of art.

1.5.3 - Create artworks using various media, techniques, and processes to communicate ideas.

2.5.1 - Describe various visual characteristics of art (e.g. sensory, formal, technical and expressive).

2.5.4 - Select and use specific visual characteristics to communicate.

5.5.1 - Compare and contrast characteristics of art.

Lesson 7 - Icons and Logos

1.5.3 - Create artworks using various media, techniques, and processes to communicate ideas.

3.5.1 - Discuss how subject matter, symbols, and ideas produce meanings in works of art.

3.5.2 - Produce a work of art that demonstrates the ability to convey meaning by integrating subject matter and symbols with ideas.

3.5.3 - Explain the way subject matter, symbols, and ideas are chosen to present meaning in student artwork.

Lesson 8 - What is Good Art?

1.5.1 - Determine differences between media, techniques or processes in works of art.

1.5.2 - Examine how different media, techniques, and processes cause different responses.

1.5.3 - Create artworks using various media, techniques, and processes to communicate ideas.

2.5.1 - Describe various visual characteristics of art (e.g. sensory, formal, technical and expressive).

2.5.2 - Identify and describe possible purposes and/or functions of art.

2.5.3 - Explain how visual characteristics, purposes, and/or functions of art may cause different responses.

2.5.4 - Select and use specific visual characteristics to communicate.

3.5.1 - Discuss how subject matter, symbols, and ideas produce meanings in works of art.

3.5.3 - Explain the way subject matter, symbols, and ideas are chosen to present meaning in student artwork.

5.5.1 - Compare and contrast characteristics of art.

5.5.2 - Identify merits in artworks.

5.5.3 - Describe meanings of art.

5.5.4 - State preferences for characteristics, merits, and meanings in art.

Made in the USA
Las Vegas, NV
24 May 2022

49290910R00066